DRAMA

Schemes, Themes & Dreams

How to plan, structure, and assess classroom events
that engage all learners

Larry Swartz

Debbie Nyman

Foreword by

David Booth

Pembroke Publishers Limited

Dedication

To Michael and Ben and Emma, with love — DN
To Lynn Slotkin oldest friend, theatre friend — LS

© 2010 Pembroke Publishers
538 Hood Road
Markham, Ontario, Canada L3R 3K9
www.pembrokepublishers.com

Distributed in the U.S. by Stenhouse Publishers
480 Congress Street
Portland, ME 04101
www.stenhouse.com

We acknowledge the financial support of the Government of Canada through the Book Publishing Industry Development Program (BPIDP) for our publishing activities.

We acknowledge the assistance of the Government of Ontario through the Ontario Media Development Corporation's Ontario Book Initiative.

Library and Archives Canada Cataloguing in Publication

Swartz, Larry
    Drama schemes, themes & dreams : how to plan, structure, and assess classroom strategies that engage young adolescent learners / Larry Swartz, Debbie Nyman.

Includes index.
ISBN 978-1-55138-253-1

    1. Improvisation (Acting)--Study and teaching (Elementary). 2. Improvisation (Acting)--Study and teaching (Middle school). 3. Drama in education. 4. Active learning. 5. Learning strategies. I. Nyman, Debbie II. Title.

PN3171.S892 2010   372.66   C2010-903823-1

Editor: Kat Mototsune
Cover Design: John Zehethofer
Typesetting: Jay Tee Graphics Ltd.

Printed and bound in Canada
9 8 7 6 5 4 3

MIX
Paper from
responsible sources
FSC
www.fsc.org   FSC® C004071

CONTENTS

Foreword

When I became a drama teacher more than forty years ago, teaching 400 Grade 7 and 8 students on a rotary timetable, there were very few books, articles, or films to draw upon in order to develop significant lessons that had depth and effect. I spent time each week scouring the library shelves, searching for scripts and poems that would work with this age group, and even more hours copying my selections onto ditto masters so that I could make hundreds of copies. All this changed during the late 1960s and through the 1970s. We began to attend workshops with drama authorities such as Brian Way, Dorothy Heathcote, Gavin Bolton, and David Davis. BEd courses were offered at several universities, with Theatre Arts as an official teaching subject, and Richard Courtney developed MEd and PhD graduate courses in Drama in Education throughout Canada. We finally had Ministry of Education Guidelines, books, and textbooks concerning the theory and practice of drama in education, and the Council of Drama in Education.

That is when I met the authors of this special book, Larry Swartz and Debbie Nyman. They were young student teachers enrolled in the Drama Option of the BEd Program at the Faculty of Education at the University of Toronto. Those were exciting years for me as an instructor in this program. I observed these two energetic and enthusiastic young people, who were excited about developing as teachers and open to new ideas about involving youngsters inside the drama frame.

Larry and Debbie graduated and became drama teachers. Over the following years, I had the good fortune to continue to work with them in their professional development programs. Whenever I was presenting a workshop, giving a talk, or participating in a conference, both of them were there, entering into the activities, asking thoughtful questions, fully involved in learning as much about teaching as they could, with drama as their mode of instruction. I began to rely on their contributions, recognizing their necessary roles in my own development as an educator, and observing their abilities to support their colleagues, to elevate the lived experience, and to strengthen the ensemble work.

When they became drama consultants in their respective school districts, we continued to work together on research projects, teacher conferences, and professional development courses. I often found them at TheatreBooks, searching for new resources, new inspiration. In the 1980s, Larry and Debbie joined our faculty at OISE as leaders in our Additional Qualification Courses in Drama, where they continue to inspire and inform teachers at both the elementary and secondary levels. I especially want to note their continuing belief in and recognition of professional theatre events as the foundation of their art form, from developing student programs and serving as board members for professional theatre companies, attending and supporting all forms of theatre—small exploratory alternative companies, contemporary theatre productions, international dance and drama festivals, school-based theatre events, Stratford and Shaw festivals, touring companies, and one-person shows. They believe in their art form.

Both Larry and Debbie continue to contribute to the drama community through their courses, their workshops and their committee work, and now, of course, with this new and engaging book. Together, they have developed these drama units by drawing upon their decades of experience of working with both beginning and experienced teachers, young people in all grades, and organizations connected to theatre and education. You will find the resources, the activities, and the strategies classroom-tested and accessible, with places and spaces for teachers to fashion these suggestions into a frame that fits the needs of their particular students. The themes, the strategies, the teaching plans, the drama extensions, will offer you resources for making drama happen in your classroom, so that your students will understand that theatre educates us in so many powerful ways. I wish I had had this book all those years ago, when drama education (and I) were just beginning. But teaching will be richer for having it today, and Larry and Debbie are to be congratulated. It has been so rewarding for me to have been part of their journey, as drama education continues to move us, to change us, to surprise us, to shock us, and most of all, to connect us.

David Booth
Professor Emeritus, OISE/University of Toronto

AN OVERVIEW

	Launching the Drama	Drama Structure using a Source	Strategy Scheme	Script Variations: Moving into Theatre	Guest Voices	Assessment
Chapter 1: Special Powers **Drama Theme:** Being Different	Name Games	*The Invisible Hunter and the Ash Maiden* (folktale)	Paired Improvisations	Ensemble Drama	• *Names as Artifacts* by Belarie Zatzman • *All In Together* by Bob Barton	Rubric for Creating and Presenting Drama Work
Chapter 2: Look in the Mirror **Drama Theme:** Identity	Games that Focus on Identity	*Speak* (novel excerpt)	Tableaux	Fragments from Canadian Plays	• *Mask and Character Development* by Teodoro Dragonieri • *Who Am I? Creating Images of Self* by Sheena Robertson	Tableaux Checklist
Chapter 3: The Bully Dance **Drama Theme:** Bullying	Circle Games to Build Inclusion	*Shame* (poem)	Choral Dramatization	Public Service Announce-ment	• *A Place for All* by Debra McLauchlan • *Building Inclusion through Drama Prompts* by Wendie Gibbons	Choral Dramatization Checklist
Chapter 4: Who Put the Words in my Mouth? **Drama Theme:** Communication	Communica-tion Games	*Persepolis* (graphic novel)	Working with Graphic Texts	Readers Theatre	• *YouTube: A New Source for Drama* by Jill Lloyd-Jones	Focus on Communication
Chapter 5: Journey to Freedom **Drama Theme:** History	Movement	*Harriet* (illustration)	Teacher in Role From Personal Voice to Theatre	Monologue	• *Moving Freely* by Lorraine Sutherns • *Drama in the Community* by Carolee Mason	Movement Rubric
Chapter 6: Home **Drama Theme:** The Refugee Experience	Games that Build Cooperation	*Tek* (fictional document)	Dialogue Script	Dialogue	• *Questioning Our Questioning* by Steve Lieberman • *Considering the Work of Augusto Boal* by Julia Balaisis	Rubric for Evaluating Role-Play
Chapter 7: Mother, What Was War? **Drama Theme:** War	Trust Games	*The Enemy* (picture book)	The Collective Creation	Interpreting Word and Song	• *Digging Deep and Bearing Witness* by Jeanie Nishimura • *From Page to Stage* by Kathleen Fraumeni	Rubric for Writing in Role
Chapter 8: Dreams Aloud **Drama Theme:** Dreams	Mime	*Alphonse* (monologue)	Revisiting, Rehaping, and Refining Scenes	Interpreting Scenes	• *Mime Workshop* by Naomi Tyrrell	Rubric for Scene Study Interpretation and Presentation Checklist

Introduction: Why This Book?

The musical *Sunday In the Park with George* by Stephen Sondheim and James Lapine tells the story of Impressionist artist George Seurat. In the opening scene the audience stares at a white stage, a white floor. The first words sung in the play serve as a metaphor for the work we do as drama teachers from day to day:

> White.
> A blank page or canvas.
> The challenge: bring order to the whole.
> Through design.
> Composition.
> Balance.
> Light.
> And harmony.

Working in the classroom in the 21st century, we are aware of the need to open the classroom doors to the issues, events, and themes, challenging and shaping our students' lives. Drama helps to convince young people that the world belongs to them and that they can affect their world in constructive ways when they engage with it. In our contemporary society, it is essential that we encourage each student to understand and to act responsibly in order to live as a caring citizen inside and outside the classroom.

Why Themes?

Exploring universal themes through drama can help students make connections to themselves and to others, and we have selected eight starting points to develop these themes that consider these human territories. Through drama, new themes will emerge. The foundation of this resource is centred on the belief that literature can be the focus and springboard of drama explorations. Themes provide a "hook" for the teacher in making connections to text and to the students we work with. Students can develop social, emotional, and cognitive skills motivated by a theme. Unpacking a theme through drama offers a myriad of possibilities for meaningful activities to enrich the creativity and thoughts of our students. Each chapter is developed on a theme: being different, identity, bullying, communication, history, the refugee experience, war, dreams. The themes from this book are drawn from a variety of literary genres, such as picture book, poetry, novel, art image, graphic text, and script.

Why Schemes?

The schemes in this book have grown out of our work with students and teachers over three decades. A scheme, a program of action, provides a framework for teachers to use material in order to shape a connected curriculum with drama at the centre. Schemes provide a system of connected elements designed to offer a thoughtful progression of verbal and nonverbal activities that move the students to understand the content, context, and themes presented in each unit. Teaching drama is about making choices, and within each scheme we suggest a number of activities to scaffold the learning. We offer teachers a range of conventions to consider in order to layer the learning and deepen engagement and understanding with their students.

In each chapter we offer Strategy Schemes that offer teachers a variety of possibilities centred on a particular drama convention. Teachers are encouraged to use these as a framework for planning, developing, and negotiating drama work as they create drama with their students. As teachers consider these suggestions, they can add to their understanding of making choices and structuring the learning. The suggestions that appear in each scheme offer a palette for teachers to create lessons, events, episodes for a brief or extended period of time.

When teaching, we never meet the same circumstances twice.
—Dorothy Heathcote, American Alliance for Theater & Education Conference (July 30, 2008; Washington DC)

Why Dreams?

In drama we invite students to bring their lives into the work, as they imagine themselves as others, as they solve problems and make meaning of challenging situations in both fictional and real worlds. We invite them to bring their stories and dreams, and through the work we hope to give them confidence and strategies to help them work toward realizing their dreams.

Dreams can be considered to be the mind's way of making sense of personal and world experiences. Throughout the book, we have woven the convention of dream-making into the drama work. When students create dream images drawn from a character, they are experiencing the poetic and symbolic potential of drama through thoughtfully selected language and gesture. Dreams also promote reflective understanding by encouraging the exploration of inner thinking, and allow groups to review the drama within the drama context. With the convention of dreams, students can draw, write, move, or dramatize a character's inner optimistic dreams or fears.

When we work in drama we often create dream worlds as we muddle about to better understand. Dream worlds are like drama worlds, places of ambiguity and mystery, often expressed in image, and always open to a myriad of possibilities and interpretations. The paths should never be linear or fixed in the here and now. Travelers in drama and dream worlds move back and forth from present to past moments; they freeze moments, extend moments, layer and re-shape moments to interpret and deepen meaning. Dreams—like the world of the theatre—rely on symbol and metaphor for understanding. It is our hope that students will better understand their own dreams as they experience the dreams and worlds of the dramas outlined in this book—the dreams of an invisible hunter, an outcast, a refugee, a traveler on a journey to freedom. In drama, real worlds and "as if" worlds collide, and in that moment teacher and students are dreammakers who stumble onto new and meaningful understandings. As Valérie Zenatti reminds us in the preface to her novel *A Bottle in the Gaza Sea*, "It is not because some people are right that others are wrong. All of our dreams must remain intact. Our dreams keep us moving forward."

Format Overview

To assist you in choosing appropriate strategies, the chapters in *Drama Schemes, Themes & Dreams* have been structured in the following way:

INTRODUCTION

- Theme overview to set the context and establish content focus for the unit
- Learning Opportunities to highlight goals and expectations as students engage in drama work

LAUNCHING THE DRAMA

- Games, movement, and/or drama activities with a skill focus
- Provides a mental set to prepare students for the theme

FRAMING THE THEME

- Focus drama learning with activities that set the stage for the content explored in the theme, helping students make connections to the theme
- Designed to stimulate the imagination and communication as students develop role-playing and improvisation skills

A DRAMA STRUCTURE

- An overview of drama episodes that describes a lesson in action over a period of time by considering drama conventions to deepen the learning
- Structure is drawn from a literary source in a particular genre

EXTENDING THE DRAMA

- Suggestions to extend the theme through writing, reading, art, technology
- Opportunities for further drama work offered to extend the thematic learning

SCRIPT VARIATIONS

- Opportunities for interpreting and improvising scripts connected to the theme
- Opportunities for students to build interpretation and move into exploring theatre forms
- Script sources include monologue, dialogue, snippets, graphic text and scenes

STRATEGY SCHEMES

- Offer a menu of suggestions for exploring a focus strategy or drama form
- Provide a framework to deepen the work and further inform the drama learning

- Can appear anywhere in the chapter, or more than once per chapter, depending on focus and form explored

ASSESSMENT PROFILES

- Rubrics, criteria checklists, and self-assessment profiles to record students' demonstration of learning

RECOMMENDED RESOURCES

See pages 169 to 173 for the recommended resources by chapter.

- Contemporary lists of literature on the themes to help build a source repertoire; include picture books, poetry, novels, nonfiction, and scripts

Guest Voices

We are grateful for the educators and artists who have shared their experiences and expertise with us in this book in the form of "guest voices." We have been fortunate to work alongside these teachers, consultants, and artists who have influenced and guided our own practice: Julia Balaisis, Bob Barton, Teodoro Dragonieri, Kathleen Fraumeni, Wendie Gibbons, Jill Lloyd-Jones, Steve Lieberman, Debra McLauchlan, Carolee Mason, Jeanie Nishimura, Sheena Robertson, Lorraine Sutherns, Naomi Tyrrell, Belarie Zatzman.

Acknowledgments

To Bob Barton for his inspired teaching and story soul;
To Jeanie Nishimura for the drama learning and the ongoing friendship;
To Kathy Lundy for helping us to teach fairly—and passionately;
To John Harvey and Leonard McHardy for filling our bookshelves;
To the Additional Qualification teaching team for their support, inspiration, and many laughs in Larry's office;
To the students we've taught, young and old, in school classrooms and university auditoria;
To David Booth for his teachings that got us started, his always-on-our shoulder-challenges, and his uplifting words that welcome readers to this book.

CHAPTER 1

Special Powers

In sharing drama we agree to live as if the story we are constructing is true.
We imagine being in the story world. We engage with it, struggle with its
unfamiliar concepts, associate our own experience with it, and fill its shape
with our own particular interpretation.
—from *Story Drama* by David Booth (2005: 14)

Drama Theme: Being Different

What does it mean to have a special power, a gift that can take you out of your
human self to a place of imagination and wonder? What if I could fly? What if I
could read minds, heal the sick, regenerate and shapeshift?

This unit is an invitation to students to imagine themselves with a special
power and, through drama and story, to explore the implications and responsibilities of living with such an extraordinary gift. And is it in fact a gift? By examining all the possibilities, students will begin to understand what it means to be
special, for the self and the community. In the context of special powers, students
will work toward becoming a community as they explore the self through name
games, explore self and other through role-playing, and explore self and the
world through story drama. Special powers is a metaphor for being different and
separate, because many young people often feel they are different and disconnected as they struggle for acceptance in a world that does not always embrace
being special.

LEARNING OPPORTUNITIES

- to begin to build a drama community through activities that invite students
  to imagine and enter the world of pretend
- to explore personal identity through drama games focusing on names
- to learn how to create authentic roles and interact in role with others
- to practice role-play in a variety of contexts and groupings
- to explore "specialness" and its implications for both the individual and society from a variety of perspectives
- to interpret a story using a variety of drama strategies
- to use drama strategies to understand the use of symbol and metaphor in
  drama work and story
- to use drama terms and language to analyze and evaluate drama work

Launching the Drama: Name Games

Names as Artifacts
by Belarie Zatzman, Associate Dean, York University

Have you ever thought about your name and what it says about you? The connection between identity and how we represent ourselves can begin to be explored through our names, which serve as markers of our identity. In many cultures, names are very significant in helping us understand where a person is from, who his/her ancestors are, or what type of qualities the family hopes that child will possess. Naming ceremonies may take place at birth (e.g., after seven days) or at a later developmental stage for confirmation or as part of a rite of passage (e.g., in African and Native American cultures). Further, the United Nations Convention on the Rights of the Child states that every child has the right to a name and an identity.

Students can tell and/or write stories about their names by considering the following prompts:

- Who were you named after?
- What does your name mean?
- Do you know your name in other languages?
- Do you have a nickname?
- Do you like your name?
- What name would you choose for yourself?
- What is an interesting (i.e., sad, funny, embarrassing) story about your name?
- How do you think your name influenced who you are?

---

1. GREETINGS

- Students move about the room, greeting each other, at first by extending a handshake.
- On a signal, each player greets in a new way: e.g., elbow to elbow, finger to finger, toe to toe, etc.

Extensions

a) Participants introduce themselves with an alliterative adjective.
b) The whole group forms a large circle. Each person takes a turn saying his/her name, coupled with a word that describes himself/herself; e.g., Lionhearted Larry, Balancing Belarie.

2. CIRCLE NAME GAME

- Each student calls out his/her name accompanied by a gesture. The group echoes the name and the gesture.
- The activity is repeated, each person using a different gesture (one that has not been used).
- A further challenge is to call out the name in a different way; i.e., loud, whisper, singing, etc.
- As a final activity, each person performs the gesture used to accompany his/her name, but does not say the name out loud.

3. GUESS WHO?

Students can learn that they have something in common with a classmate, or they learn something interesting about someone that might otherwise have taken all year to discover.

- Distribute index cards to each student. Each student independently writes one little-known fact about himself/herself on the card. It should be something that people could not know just by looking at them. Students' names should NOT appear on the cards.
- Cards are collected and shuffled. As each card is read out loud in turn, invite the class to guess who the fact describes.
- The activity could be repeated on another day with students listing new facts, or two facts per card.

4. SPELL YOUR NAME: MOVEMENT

Participants work independently, using their hands to spell their names in a variety of ways:

- using a pointing finger
- using a large paintbrush
- using spaghetti
- using a small toothpick
- using elbows
- using whole body

Extension

Students work in pairs. Repeating some of the movement activities, pairs mirror each other's movements. Music accompaniment can be added to this activity

5. TOSS BALL/NAME CALL

- Students stand in a circle. To begin, a ball is given to one player, who calls his/her name and tosses it to someone else in the circle. The ball continues to be passed, ensuring that all become familiar with names.
- The activity is repeated. This time, students start with their hands folded in front of them; after tossing the ball to someone else in the circle, students place their hands behind their backs. In this way, each person passes (and receives) the ball once.
- The activity is repeated once again, following the sequence of passing the ball. Draw the students' attention to the pattern that has been established.

Extensions

a) Challenge students to complete the activity in a time limit.
b) Students pass the ball, but do not call out names.
c) The pattern of passing the ball is reversed. The ball is tossed from last person to first person.
d) Two balls are passed, one using the original pattern, and one using the reverse pattern.
e) Students find a new spot in the circle. The game is repeated.
f) Additional balls are added (up to five).

g) Students toss silly objects instead of a ball: e.g., a rubber chicken, a stuffed toy.

h) A number of balls are tossed about randomly. Students do not have to use the original pattern, but call out the name of a player and then toss the ball.

6. NAME AEROBICS

- Students write their first names on a card as an acrostic: for each letter of the name, a verb is chosen or an exercise movement is described; e.g. for SANDY, S = slide, A = arm lift, N = nine jumping jacks, D = dance, Y = yawn.
- Students practice a physical routine by performing each of the exercises listed in their names.
- Students can exchange cards and practice a routine by performing the exercises listed in their partners' names.

Extension

Students work in groups. Each person has a chance to be the leader to instruct others about the exercises using the verbs of their name.

Framing the Theme: Invitations to Pretend

LET'S IMAGINE!

Having students fill in the Let's Imagine questionnaire on page 15 invites them into the world of pretend. Students complete each of the statements and then, in pairs or small groups, compare responses. Encourage students in their discussions to share reasons for their answers.

Alternatively, students can wander about the room and find twelve people to interview. In this way, students can complete the questionnaire by filling one blank apiece. Students can sign their name to each of the items, or students can share their responses in a circle by identifying answers that have been recorded on this sheet; e.g., I know that Brendan would like to meet Winston Churchill.

Extensions

a) Students transform into the animal (still image, movement, sound).
b) Students hum or sing the favorite song.
c) Partners interview in role as the famous character or person from the past.
d) Students tell a story about visiting a special environment.
e) Students share facts they know about a country that they wish to visit.
f) Students mime an activity that shows the special power they've chosen.

INVITATIONS TO ROLE-PLAY

The following series of dramatic activities invites students to step into role and enter imagined worlds. When role-playing, we encourage students to find a place where self and other meet to create authenticity. Teachers need to help students find a balance between who they are and the imagined character they play by speaking, using language and gesture to express thoughts, feelings, and attitudes beyond superficial and stereotyped representations.

Let's Imagine

If I could be an ANIMAL, I'd be a _____.

If I could be a COLOR, I'd be _____.

If I could be a NUMBER, I'd be _____.

If I could be a SONG, I'd be _____.

If I could be a COUNTRY, I'd be _____.

If I were a FLAVOR, I'd be _____.

If I could be a FAMOUS PERSON , I'd be _____.

If I could meet ANYONE FROM THE PAST, I would choose _____.

If I could explore a special ENVIRONMENT in the outdoor world, I would

explore _____.

If I could TRANSFORM, I would become a _____.

If I could do one thing to HELP THE WORLD, it would be to _____.

If I could wake up tomorrow with a SPECIAL POWER, it would be the power

of _____.

Pembroke Publishers ©2010 *Drama Schemes, Themes & Dreams* by Larry Swartz and Debbie Nyman ISBN 978-1-55138-253-1

In this unit, students invent special powers and work in role to make these powers seem real. Because the students are given the freedom to create talents, skills, and stories that are often connected to the world of fantasy, they are given opportunities to practice being experts and behaving as if these stories were believable and part of the here and now.

IMAGINE A SETTING: MIME TO ROLE-PLAY

- Working in groups of four, students number themselves 1 to 4.
- Call each student 1 out of the room and give a particular setting to create through mime: e.g., shoe store, factory, office, snowboarding hill, art studio, fast-food restaurant, skating rink, rock concert, school dance, etc.
- The student comes back to the group and mimes actions in this setting.
- When the others in the group think they know where and what is going on, they enter the scene and begin miming actions.
- When everyone is in the scene, the students begin to speak in the scene in role.
- When everyone is participating and speaking, ask the groups to freeze.
- Students share with each other how they figured out the scene, which actions were revealing, the roles they chose to play.
- The activity continues with each student 2 setting a new scene.

EXPERT

- Model the role-play by becoming the expert for the whole class to interview.
- Working in groups of four, students number themselves 1 to 4. Student 1 plays the role of the expert and the other students play the interested parties described in the scenarios listed below.
- You can ask questions of the group at the end of each role-play to report the learning to the class.
- The scenarios could also be continued to build a drama structure. For example, the expert time-traveler scenario could begin a drama on the implications of time travel.

In one experiment, four-year-old children were asked to stand still for as long as they could. They typically did not make it past a minute. But when the kids played a make-believe game in which they were guards at a factory, they were able to stand at attention for more than four minutes.
—from "The Make-Believe Solution" by Paul Tough (2009: 24)

1. Time-Travel Expert

The group has come to find out more about time travel as they are putting together a mission to travel in time. They want to know about different traveling devices, the kind of people they should choose to travel, the recording devices used to remember the mission, etc.

Teacher Prompts
- to the time-travelers: Do you want to participate in this mission given what you know about their plans? Why or why not?
- to the mission planners: Do you think this time-traveler would be suitable for your mission? Why or why not?

2. Robot Expert

Expert is meeting with a group of parents and principals to inform them of and ask permission to try out the latest robot, the robot teacher. Students and parents will want to know more about the robot's ability to teach, discipline, and care for the students.

Teacher Prompts

- to the groups of parents and principals: Do you have any concerns about the robot teacher? Are you considering trying out the product? Why or why not? Why do you think the robot teacher is a good idea?
- To robot expert: How might you improve your robot design and capabilities? What is the most unique thing about your robot?

3. Expert on Water Supplies

Some additional experts:
- Lion tamer
- Magician who can make things disappear
- Paper-clip designer
- Underwater explorer
- Author on Wikipedia

This scenario takes place 50 years in the future. The expert is meeting with a group of scientists who want to transport water from Mars to Earth, as the Earth's water supply is in danger. The scientists need to know about the water and the availability of it on Mars, how to ask for it and transport it.

Teacher Prompts

- to the scientists: Do you feel it is possible to transport the water? What is the greatest challenge in this endeavor?
- to the water experts: Do you think the people on the Earth should go ahead with this? Do you see any dangers? Do the Earth people have a right to the water on Mars?

4. Expert on Teenagers

The expert has created a monitoring device for adolescents, a minuscule chip that is embedded under the skin that will track the kid at all times. The expert is meeting with parents of teenagers who are considering the product. They will need to know if it has been tested, if the subjects are informed, and how to use the device.

Teacher Prompts

- to the parents: Why might you consider this product? What are the advantages? What are your concerns?
- to the expert: Do you feel parents are ready to use this product? What plans should be made to consult with teenagers?

PAIRED IMPROVISATION: INTERVIEW/ROLE-PLAY

- Working in pairs, students decide who is A and B.
- Describe the scenario to the students: "You are adult friends who have been very, very good friends since childhood. A has asked B to meet tonight to talk about something very important." It is useful to reinforce the friendship so that students will accept the information.
- Instruct the B partners to create a set for the two to meet, while the A partners receive secret information about the role.
- Give the A partners secret information on cards or inform them in a group away from the B partners:

  You have a special power that is not visible. You have had this power since you were a child, but you have rarely used it—only for good and only in desperate situations. You have never told anyone about this power before tonight. Something has changed in your life and you need advice about the power. Perhaps you have less control over the power or maybe you are feeling that you should use it or share it. You are going to disclose to this friend and ask for advice on how to continue living with this special power. Find a way to tell them so that they will believe you. Do not use or try to demonstrate your power. You must try to convince them only through your words.

You are crazy to know who I am
I'll show you who I am and what I am
The secret of invisibility lies in my books
I shall offer my secret to the world with all its terrible power
Even the moon is frightened of me
— from *The Invisible Man,* the movie, 1933

- Give the students a moment to select a special power, such as extraordinary strength, the ability to fly, invisibility, etc. Ask the students to tell you their choices before the role-play begins.
- Students role-play until you give a signal to end. You will want to listen in on the groups and side coach as they work to determine when the role-play should end.
- Students form two circles: B partners sit in the inside and the A partners on the outside behind their partners.
- Teacher interviews B partners: What did your friend tell you this evening? What advice did you give? What are you worried about? Did you help your friend feel better? Is there anything you wish you had said to your friend?
- Students change places and teacher interviews the A partners: Was your friend helpful? How do you feel now that you have told someone? What do you plan on doing now?

Strategy Scheme: Paired Improvisation — What Next?

Here are ten strategies that can be used after paired improvisations. These strategies are particularly useful if students are working in the context of interview situations. In pairs, one person will be the interviewee/storyteller who is providing information, and one is the interviewer who is learning facts and seeking clarification by asking questions.

1. Interviewers stand. They report what they have heard to the teacher working in role.
2. Storytellers stand. They report their story to the teacher working in role.
3. Partners switch roles and repeat the improvisation.
4. Interviewers stand, find a new sitting partner, and report what they have learned from the interview (possibly in role as the storyteller).
5. Storytellers, interviewers, or both conduct a meeting to share stories; e.g., a press conference, an editorial meeting, or a city council meeting.
6. Storytellers and interviewers work together to create a tableau image that encapsulates the story that was told. As an extension, they might create two additional tableaux to show what happened before, and what might happen next.
7. Partners enact the paired improvisation while audience members watch to learn new information about a character. This can be extended to a hot-seating activity in which the group asks questions of one of the characters.
8. The interview is conducted in some future time to determine how a problem is unfolding or being solved.
9. A third person is added as a witness who reports what was discussed or is given a role to contribute to the interview.
10. The information provided in the interview is used as a context for writing in role. Students might write a letter, a report, or a diary entry from a character's point of view.

SPECIAL POWERS STATUES

- The B partners consider a special power they would like to explore and create a statue in the role of a person using this special power; e.g., a statue of being in flight or shapeshifting. A partners turn away from B partners while they create the statues.
- When B is frozen, A creates the mirror image of the statue.
- Both statues unfreeze, and A interviews B to find out as much as possible about this power.
- On a signal from the teacher, B partners freeze again; each A partner stands in front of a new B and takes the new position. Again A and B unfreeze, and A interviews B to learn more about the power.

LIMITATIONS AND POSSIBILITIES: CREATING A THEATRE PIECE

- Discuss with the class how a special power might be limiting or freeing: How would it change your life? Would it make your life better or more challenging?
- Students brainstorm and record their thoughts and feelings on having a special power on two pieces of chart paper with the titles *Limitations* and *Possibilities*.
- Invite students to closely examine both pieces of chart paper and choose one to further explore, signaling their choice by standing around that paper. Some students might want to stand in the place between the two choices, and they can form a third group.
- Students work in their groups to create a theatre piece communicating the limitations or possibilities of the special power. Each group will select three words or phrases from the paper, create one image for each, insert the words into the image, and create and practice transitions between the images.
- Students can also use words as transitions. The class can negotiate an order for the presentations and share the theatre pieces.

Reflection

- How does drama help us to understand the power of special powers?
- What was easy about inventing a special power?
- What was challenging about inventing a special power?
- Students can share with the opposite group the images and words that stood out or were particularly effective in communicating that element of special powers.

THE SPECIAL POWERS INSTITUTE: WHOLE-CLASS IMPROVISATION

- This drama will begin with you in the role of the head of the Institute of Special Powers and students in the roles of parents of children with special powers. The teacher in role addresses the students in role:

  I have asked you to come here today because I know that you have special children and I—that is, we—want to help you. We know that there are many challenges raising children with special powers and so we know you will be very interested in our Institute of Special Powers. We will take your children and educate them to develop their full potential at our Institute. We will bring them all together. We have the finest teachers, equipment, and technology, much more than you or any public school could offer your children.

- At this point, continuing in role, you can take questions from students. The students will ask about financial considerations, possible payment, and eventually about the location—or you can introduce this information.

  The school is a residential school and, because of the potential danger of the powers involved, the location cannot be given to anyone. It could be dangerous for others in the world to know these special children are together.

- Then ask the parents if they would be willing to send their children to the school.

Extensions

a) **Discussion out of role:** Students discuss the situation out of role, considering their concerns, why the school is a good idea, how they might proceed, whether or not parents should consult with their children, etc. In pairs they could make a plan for how they want to proceed.

b) **Hot-seating:** The group might decide that they want further information and discuss who might provide the information: teachers at the school, administrators, students presently enrolled. They could role-play these people, or you could role-play one of these people, for the group to hot-seat to gather more information before they decide.

c) **Creating the school:** Students divide into two groups and create the school or a part of it using furniture and props in the classroom space. After planning and rehearsing, each group takes the other group on a tour of the school they have created.

d) **Brochures:** Students could create brochures of the school and share with the parent group. What message(s) will they include to promote the school? What visual images will be included to invite others to consider registering for this school?

e) **Journal Entry of a Special Person:** Students can write journal entries in the role of the person with a special power. Have them think about

  - the moment you discovered you had this power
  - the first time you used the power
  - a time you were almost discovered using the power
  - a day you vowed to never use it again
  - a day at the Special Powers Institute

f) **SPP (Special Power Person) Letters:** In role, students can write a letter
  - to another person who has just discovered his/her special power
  - to a parent describing the school and the student's feelings about being there
  - from a parent to a child with special powers describing why the parent chose to send or not send the child to the special school

Reflection

- Ask students to consider how their thinking about special powers has changed through the drama, from the initial role-play to this whole-class drama.

- Invite students to think about what this drama is *really about* and record their thoughts on another piece of chart paper with the title *This Drama Is About _____ for Me*.
- After students have recorded their ideas, invite them to discuss how special powers is a metaphor, and how we learn through metaphor. This might also be a prompt for a personal journal response.

A Drama Structure Using an Aboriginal Tale

REMEMBERING A MOMENT: THINK–WRITE–PAIR–SHARE

Students were asked to think of a time when they felt invisible to others, not seen, not heard, and not listened to, as though they were not there at all. Students could, if they wished, consider a time that they wished they were invisible to others: they were asked to describe what someone would have seen had they been visible in this moment to just that one person; they were also asked to consider who they would choose be visible to in this moment. Students then wrote these memories and thoughts on index cards and shared with a partner. Several students volunteered to share their stories with the whole group.

THE INVISIBLE HUNTER AND THE ASH MAIDEN: TEACHER READ-ALOUD AND DISCUSSION

An eloquent picture book version of this Cinderella story is presented in *The Rough-Face Girl* by Rafe Martin, illustrated by David Shannon.

See "The Invisible Hunter and the Ash Maiden" on page 22. This story is a variant of a popular tale told in many Aboriginal peoples with languages in the Algonquin family.

The teacher read the story aloud to the students. The class discussed the story, thinking about and responding to the following questions:

- Where would you place yourself if you were inside the story?
- What did this story invite you to wonder about?
- In what ways did this story remind you of other stories? movies?

WHOOSH!

(with thanks to Jonothan Neelands for sharing)

Whoosh! is a spontaneous storytelling activity that involves using the body to actively represent and portray people, objects, and scenery that comprise a story that is told/read out loud. The teacher told "The Invisible Hunter and the Ash Maiden," pausing to signal to the group to enter the circle and bring to life the part of the story that has just been revealed. Without any negotiation, students entered to physicalize the story. The teacher continued with the story, and signaled for others to enter and depict what is being told. When the circle became too overcrowded, the teacher called out, "Whoosh! Whoosh! Whoosh!"; this signified everyone to clear the space and return to the circle. The storytelling continued uninterrupted.

TELL ME: RETELLING

The students worked in pairs, describing to a partner a moment that they clearly visualized while listening to the story. They described a moment where they

The Invisible Hunter and the Ash Maiden

Long ago, in a village by the woods, lived a hunter. A brave, successful, and said-to-be handsome hunter with a special power—the power of invisibility. No one had ever seen the Invisible Hunter. No one had ever met the Invisible Hunter face-to-face, except for his sister, who lived with him in a wigwam by the lake. The other hunters kept their distance from the Hidden Hunter. The women of the village, however, hoped to catch a glimpse of him, for it was said that if he became visible to a woman, she would become his bride.

Young maidens would make their way to the great wigwam decorated with the sun, the stars, and a rainbow. The Invisible Hunter's sister, known as Patient One, would test the maidens who came one-by-one with the hopes of marriage. And, one-by-one, they sadly departed, because they failed to truly see the invisible hero.

In that same village, there lived three sisters who had lost their mother. The youngest sister had a gentle heart, but the older two were known for their jealous and cruel natures. Each day when their father went out hunting, Middle Sister would make the Youngest Sister sit by the fire pit and feed the flames. Older Sister would hold the girl down and lay a burning branch on her cheeks.

"If you tell father what I've done you will be sorry!" warned Middle Sister.

"How ugly you are! Your face is covered with ashes," mocked Older Sister.

Each night when the father came home, he would ask his youngest child, "Why are you burnt again?"

Middle Sister would interject, "Father, she always disobeys you. She was playing with fire, even though you have warned her many times. I tried to stop her!"

"Is this true?" the father would ask, turning to his youngest daughter She would hang her head, bite her lip, and remain silent.

Day after day, the older girls continued to torment their sister. They forced her to tend the fire, and more ashen scars appeared on her face. They forced her to wear rags. They cut off her singed braids.

One day, Ash Maiden watched her older sisters putting on fine buckskin dresses, strings of beads, and the finest of feathers to adorn their hair. She looked at her sisters with envy.

"One of us is going to marry Invisible One! That is something you can never dream of."

"Your place is here in this wigwam!"

Ash Maiden hung her head in despair as the two departed.

That afternoon, the sisters reached the wigwam by the edge of the forest. Patient One came out to greet them.

"We've come to marry the Hunter," both sisters called together.

"If you want to marry my brother you will have to see him. He is making his way now from the woods."

"We will see him," said Middle Sister.

"We know how strong and tall he is," said Older Sister. "There is no one as handsome as your brother."

Pembroke Publishers ©2010 *Drama Schemes, Themes & Dreams* by Larry Swartz and Debbie Nyman ISBN 978-1-55138-253-1

Patient One asked, "What color is the feather in his hair?

Older Sister looked hard in the distance and, not seeing anyone, guessed. "His feather? It is the white feather of an eagle."

"And his bowstring, what is it made of?" asked Patient One.

"His bowstring? It is a strip of braided rawhide!" Middle Sister stammered.

"And the bow?"

"A willow branch."

"Liars! You do not see my brother!" Patient One frowned.

"We do, we have," the two persisted together. "You ask such silly questions! Your test is not fair!"

Giving the two maidens a second chance, Patient One took them to a place furthest from the entrance of the great wigwam. Just then, a breath could be heard. A deep voice called out, "Good evening, sister!"

The two sisters jumped in surprise, stared at the doorway, but still could see no one.

"Greetings, my brother!"

Middle Sister's eyes widened as a rust-colored moccasin flew through the air and dropped to the floor, followed by another. Older Sister gasped as a great bow and beaded arrows appeared in the air and were set down before her. Moments later, scraps of food rose from the wooden tray near the fire and disappeared into an invisible mouth.

Tense and nervous, Middle Sister asked, "Which one of us will you choose?"

Older Sister bravely stood, "When shall we wed?"

"Wed?! What makes you think my brother would marry deceitful cheaters like you?"! exclaimed Patient One. "Leave at once!"

The two sisters, ashamed and in tears, left the wigwam and headed home.

The next day the two remained quiet as they went about their daily chores. Little Ash Maiden, however, was speaking to her father. "May I please have new buckskin clothing and beaded moccasins? I am off to marry the Hidden One."

"Have you seen him?"

"Wherever I look, I see his face."

"Daughter, I am sorry. I have no beads for you, no buckskin. The only moccasins I have are my own cracked pair that I have worn for two years. I'm sure they will be too big for you."

"Father, I will take whatever you are so kind to give me." Ash Maiden took the old pair of moccasins and put them on her own tiny feet. She wrapped birch bark around her like a shawl and she set out to the woods of the Invisible Hunter.

The two sisters suddenly took notice of all that was going on. As the young girl headed toward the woods, Middle Sister called out, "Are those slippers big enough for you?"

"Is it fun to be dressed like a tree?" Older Sister mocked.

Pembroke Publishers ©2010 *Drama Schemes, Themes & Dreams* by Larry Swartz and Debbie Nyman ISBN 978-1-55138-253-1

Ash Maiden ignored their taunts and laughter and walked on through the village, where she was met with the taunts and laughter of the villagers. "Look at her. No one should be seen wearing those clothes, walking in those moccasins."

She held her head up and continued until she reached the wigwam at the end of the village. She was greeted by Patient One, who welcomed her warmly.

"I've come to marry the Hunter!" declared Ash Maiden.

Patient One took kindly to Ash Maiden and offered her an evening meal. When the sun set, the hunter's sister led her to the edge of the woods. "Here comes my brother. Tell me if you see him."

Ash Maiden gazed ahead and answered, "I'm not sure but..." Suddenly her eyes grew in wonder. "Yes! Oh, yes. He is as I have seen him in my mind's eye, in my dreams. His face is handsome, his eyes are kind."

"I will ask you some questions," said Patient One. "First, what color is the feather in his hair?"

Ash Maiden answered, "His feather? It is a raven's feather, black as night."

"And his bowstring, what is it made of?"

"His bowstring? It is a strap of tiny white stars. Like the Milky Way."

"And his bow?"

"His bow? Why it is the great curve of the rainbow."

Patient One smiled with delight. "Let us return!"

In the wigwam, Patient One opened a chest and pulled out buckskin, soft and golden. As she slipped it over Ash Maiden's body, a deep voice called out, "Greetings, my sister."

Ash Maiden turned to face the entrance and gazed at the mighty hunter. Their eyes met with admiration.

"Greetings, brother," replied his sister. "You are revealed."

The hunter walked over to Ash Maiden and took her hands in his. As he held them, the ash scars on the girl's face vanished. Her skin grew smooth again and her braids reappeared, rich and black. "I have waited many moons to find a woman so pure of heart and brave of spirit. Only then would I become visible."

And the one who had been hidden for so many years stepped forward and asked the beautiful young maiden who had also been hidden for so many years, "Will you be my bride?"

Pembroke Publishers ©2010 *Drama Schemes, Themes & Dreams* by Larry Swartz and Debbie Nyman ISBN 978-1-55138-253-1

In his book *Tell Me Another*, master storyteller Bob Barton provides teachers with an excellent resource that helps teachers tell and teach storytelling techniques.

would have liked to been inside the story to speak to a character. They shared what they would have said to the character.

The students worked in groups of four, numbering themselves 1 to 4. Number 1 began retelling the story. On a signal from the teacher, number 2 continued the retelling, and then 3, and then 4.

The students repeated the activity but retold the story *in role* from a chosen character's perspective. As the students worked, changing storytellers, the teacher circulated listening for students telling in role with commitment. The teacher signaled the rest of the class to freeze, listened in on a particular group for a few moments, and then had the class resume. This was repeated a few times to give the students strong models to encourage them.

WHAT'S THE STORY?: STILL IMAGES TO WORDS

The students discussed: What is this story about for you? What are the main themes of the story? Through the discussion they generated a list of words, including *love, hidden, abuse, truth, patience, courage*. Working in groups of four or five, students created a moment from the story in two tableaux with a transition to depict the word. They chose where to insert and say the word in the images. The students then shared the images and words. They analyzed the images and discussed how some groups had created the same moment to interpret different words. They discussed the issues of the story through the presentations. Students added new words to the original list in response to the tableaux presentations.

HIDDEN SCENES: SMALL-GROUP IMPROVISATION

Working in small groups, students brainstormed scenes that they felt were missing in the story, scenes that would give them further information and understanding of the story. They selected one and created a brief scene. The scene began in a tableau, came to life for a few minutes with dialogue and narration, and ended in a tableau. The scenes they chose to create developed how the hunter came to be invisible, the death of the mother, the fate of the sisters. Students explored the challenge of depicting invisibility theatrically in their scenes of how the hunter was given the special power.

To present the scenes, groups gathered in a circle in their opening position and the teacher acted as a conductor, signaling a group to begin the improvisation and to fade out as she signaled another group to begin. The teacher returned to groups to continue where they left off. This continued until all the groups had more or less completed their scenes, with some groups beginning their scenes a second time. Using this strategy encouraged the students to hear the different voices and interpretations of the missing stories as a collage of impressions.

Reflection

Students discussed the scenes considering the following:

- What did you further learn about the characters and the meaning of the story?
- Describe an image or moment from a scene that was effective. Give reasons for your choice.
- Describe how it felt to be ready in your own scene, knowing you could be called upon again and watching the other scenes at the same time.

TO BE (OR NOT): WHOLE-CLASS IMPROVISATION

The teacher entered the drama in the role of the elder in the village and the students were in the role of villagers. In role, the teacher addressed the villagers:

> The Invisible Hunter has revealed himself to the Ash Maiden and they have married.
> We have heard the stories of his amazing gifts—his feather, bowstring, and bow.
> We have heard that he was able to heal her scars with a touch of his hand. And now we wonder, will they reveal themselves to us, will they share their powers and gifts? Would we be able to convince them?

The students responded in role and decided they wanted to convince the Hunter and Maiden to be part of the community and share their gifts. They wanted to know more about the power of invisibility and to use it to hunt. They decided this would be advantageous to them. They brought forth several plans and strategies, including having the sisters apologize and ask the Maiden for forgiveness, offering them gifts from the villagers, giving a party to celebrate their wedding, etc. They agreed to invite the Hunter and the Maiden to the meeting to persuade them by first apologizing and then offering them the benefits of being part of a community.

Two students volunteered to play the Hunter and the Maiden and to come before the villagers. Two students volunteered to play the sisters. Students volunteered to play the hunters. Together the villagers tried to convince the Hunter to share his gifts, to live amongst the villagers with the maiden.

CULMINATING ACTIVITY: CORRIDOR OF VOICES

The villagers created a corridor by standing and facing each other. The Hunter began walking from one entrance to the corridor and the Maiden began walking from the other entrance. As they moved through the corridor, the villagers gave them advice and reasons to re-enter the village together. When the Hunter and the Maiden met in the middle, the teacher asked them if they would come back to reveal themselves and live amongst the people. In our drama, they agreed to interact with the village, but to continue to live outside the village, partly hidden; they asked for their privacy to be respected.

Reflection

- The teacher asked the students playing the Hunter and the Maiden to share how they felt walking through the corridor. What did they hear that helped them make their choices? What words were comforting?
- The class also discussed: What was the drama about now? What did the drama remind them of? What did they learn about the real world by role-playing in this fictional world?

Extending the Drama

STORY THEATRE

Have students prepare a story theatre presentation of this tale. Students decide which character roles they will each be playing. A narrator or narrators can be designated to tell the story, or the characters can serve as both narrators and characters within the story. Inanimate objects can take a role and speak. The story can be divided into different sections and assigned to small groups to perform. Story theatre makes use of simple settings and properties. Songs, sound effects, tableaux, and movement can enhance a presentation. Story theatre is a suitable format for older students to work with younger students.

WRITING A MONOLOGUE

Students write a monologue in the role of a character or object to express their version of the story. They could focus on one event in the story instead of retelling the whole plot. Students can share excerpts of the monologue aloud with the class.

LETTERS OF APOLOGY

Invite the students to write a letter of apology to the Maiden in the role of one of the sisters or as a villager who ridiculed her as she made her way to the Hunter.

FURTHER RETELLING

Students can retell the story through another form, such as a poem, song, or graphic representation. Students can illustrate a scene from the story through visual arts.

INVESTIGATING CINDERELLA STORIES

The Invisible Hunter and the Ash Maiden is a version of the Cinderella story. Ask students to research Cinderella stories from other cultures and retell one version to the class. Students can also discuss the similarities and differences in the versions, and consider what we learn about the particular culture from the story.

INVISIBLE PEOPLE IN THE WORLD TODAY

I am an invisible man. I am a man of substance, of flesh, bone and liquid. I might even be said to possess a mind. I am invisible simply because people refuse to see me.
— from *Invisible Man* by Ralph Ellison

Discuss invisible people in the world today. Ask the students to consider who in our society is hidden or invisible to the world. Who does not have a voice in decisions about their lives and the world? Working in small groups and looking back at the writing they did in the first activity, students select and use a scene to explore an individual or group that is invisible or hidden in our society. In the scene, students should describe who is invisible, why they are hidden or invisible, and how we can change this situation, give them a voice, and make them visible. Students can research statistics about this situation or group and include the data in the scene. Students can give the scene a title and share with the class.

Script Variation: Ensemble Drama

All In Together
by Bob Barton, drama educator, storyteller

One chilly autumn evening in the late 1960s, David Booth and I had the pleasure of participating in a workshop led by the late poet and playwright, James Reaney.

Dr. Reaney dropped a large stack of newspapers on the floor in front of the one hundred or so participants, and announced that we were going to create a play about newspaper. We were to wear newspaper, use newspaper for sound effects, create art objects of newspaper, dance newspaper, sing newspaper, and create text about newspaper.

He divided us into groups of 20, each with a different assignment. One group was to create a movement piece depicting frenzy and urgency, as machines and humans fed the huge printing presses of the era to churn out the daily news.

Another group was to create a choral composition based on newspaper jargon, everything from the cries of newsfolk hawking papers on street corners—"Extra! Extra! Read all about it!"— to the lingo inside the plant—"Stop the presses!"

A props group had to think of all the uses to which old newspapers could be put: e.g., insulation, wrap; artifacts such as paper hats, boats, kites, dresses; and structural tubes to create forms. Objects were to be created and accompanied by an "ode to newspapers."

The music group was to compose a ballad based on the classified ads; a set-design group was to create the ambiance of a large city using only flashlights.

Groups were given one hour to complete the work. When the groups reassembled, Dr. Reaney asked each group to present its work. Next we discussed the order in which we wanted the groups to perform. The performance was to be seamless, so the ballad group was called upon to provide the links between scenes. A chant from the choral group was paired with the movement piece.

An opening and a closing were shaped and the play unfolded. The closing involved all of us making wind sounds and flapping sheets of newspaper to portray the demise of old newspapers as they were flung about, ghosts of their former selves, on the back of gusting winds.

Afterwards, David and I asked Dr. Reaney what he called the activity. He shrugged and said, "Just a play." Subsequently David and I decided to call the activity *Ensemble Drama* because it involved many players working together to improvise a living text with a potential script emerging from, rather than predetermining, the final project. Ensemble Drama provides an opportunity for a large group of students to participate in dramatic presentation. The group, which can vary from 20 to 100 members, pools its artistic and creative responses and develops a unique, spontaneous, dramatic event through the integration of drama, dance, music, and the visual arts.

Dr. Reaney's work with us had been bold, playful, high-risk, and exciting. In subsequent years, to make the concept easier to manage for a teacher on his or her own, we found that a narrative line was a big help with the structuring. Among the narratives that adapted nicely to ensemble work were bare-bones tales such as those found in ballads and ancient world myths.

Also, some classes required more support than others with the group work. In such instances, each assignment was worked through with the whole class, then parceled out to groups for the performance.

Here is an example of how an ensemble drama might be planned based on a folktale. There are many stories about Quat, the solar god of the Banks Islands north of the New Hebrides in Melanesia, but one of my personal favorites is the story of how Quat found night. (A version of this story appears in *In the Beginning* by Virginia Hamilton.)

The Power of Night
"In the beginning, there was light. It never dimmed, this light over everything. It was bright—all light everywhere and there was no rest from it."

Quat had eleven brothers who complained to him about the light.

So Quat loaded a pig into his canoe and journeyed to the far edge of the sky to the place called Qong, Night.

"Night was dark. It had no light anywhere in it. It touched Quat's eyes and gave him the blackest eyebrows. It taught him sleep as well."

Quat traded Night his pig for a piece of darkness and paddled home. But Night followed him and, for the first time, the sun slipped down toward the west.

"Look the sun is going," said the brothers. "Will it return again?"

The brothers were frightened by the darkness and Quat taught them how to prepare for night and how to sleep.

"I think we must be dying," said the brothers.

"It is just sleep," said Quat. "That's what it is called."

When night had lasted long enough, the birds signaled the end by whistling, chirping and squawking.

"Then Quat took a red stone and cut a hole in Night. The first light that came out of that tear was red light. And then all of the light shone brightly."

This elliptical tale has great potential for elaboration as an ensemble drama. Here are suggestions for the group assignments:

Choral Speaking: "In the beginning, there was light"

Create a choral speaking selection to describe the world under constant light.

1. Begin by listing all the expressions you can think of to describe unrelenting light; e.g., light everywhere, bright light, everywhere light, over everything light, etc.
2. Create a six-line piece, using short sharp lines.
3. Divide the work with solos and unison parts.
4. Now do the same for Night.

Improvisation Group: Learning To Sleep

Create a short scene in which Quat teaches his family about sleep.

- What will they need to learn? (how to make a bed, how to lie down etc.)
- What questions will the family have?
- What emotions will they experience?
- What conflict might occur? (Is Night too frightening? Do they want Quat to return it?)

Alternatively, students could perform a series of short monologues in which members of Quat's family tell about their first experience with the great darkness, the first sleep, the first sunrise, the first dreams.

Music Group: Night comes, we sleep; day breaks, we wake

Using musical instruments, sound makers, and body or vocal sounds, create an overture for Finding Night that contains three movements:

1. The quest into the unknown to find night.
2. Learning to sleep: this could be a new lullaby set to a familiar tune or be an entirely new creation.
3. The first sunrise: the tearing of the fabric of night and the sounds of birds would be important elements.

Movement Group: And the great darkness, Night, gave Quat a piece of itself.

Create a movement/dance piece in which Quat encounters the great darkness.

- How does it affect Quat at first?
- How does Quat create a relationship with Night?
- How does Quat obtain a piece of the darkness?

Tips on Preparing Ensemble Drama

- Allow 45 minutes to an hour for the group work. When the whole group reconvenes, the students will have the raw material for a performance piece.
- You might have each group preview its work to the whole group then invite the students to shape the sequence, choreography, and direction of the piece. Any additional connecting material can be developed now and worked into the next run-through.
- You can suggest a rough sequence to the students, then improvise the order and direction of events as they unfold. Now that they've seen what is possible, the students might wish to do additional work on their own segments or suggest new material to enhance the overall effect.
- Ensemble drama places a high priority on cooperation and sharing, as students work to support, sustain, and strengthen the collective effort. The spontaneity that is called upon, with its blending of the various arts, can lift drama into new forms of expression and a pleasurable, rewarding drama event.

Assessment: Rubric For Creating and Presenting Drama Work

	Limited	Satisfactory	Good	Excellent
CREATING • uses a variety of drama forms to plan, generate, and focus the work • experiments and investigates possibilities, and contributes ideas • plans and shapes the drama through negotiation of ideas • is willing to revisit, revise, and refine the work				
PRESENTING • selects and combines elements of drama to create dramatic effect • is aware of audience and adopting appropriate tone and means of presentation • provides feedback to others • accepts feedback from teacher and peers in order to create and present				
REFLECTING AND ANALYZING • reflects on personal learning • interprets and analyzes the works of others • applies critical analysis process to communicate understandings • analyzes and describes using drama terminology				

Pembroke Publishers ©2010 *Drama Schemes, Themes & Dreams* by Larry Swartz and Debbie Nyman ISBN 978-1-55138-253-1

CHAPTER 2

Look in the Mirror

I looked in the mirror
And what did I see?
A real handsome dude
Looking just like me.
—from *Looking Like Me* by Walter Dean Myers

Drama Theme: Identity

"Who am I?" Throughout our lives, we question our identities, our relationships with others, and our place in the world, but it is during the years of adolescence that we search for answers to questions about the self. As teenagers, we look into the mirror to find out who we are, and the answers may be both fuzzy and sharpened at the same time. During adolescence, everybody wants to be the same and nobody wants to be different—and then in a moment it all changes and everyone wants to be different. Adolescence is a time of belonging—or not.

This theme invites students to gaze into mirrors, look through the window, and open doors to consider who they are and who they are becoming. Growing into adulthood is a challenging journey that young people undertake. Drama provides opportunities for them to see their reflections with more purpose and clarity. Drama helps students plot the course to maturity and helps them find that they are not alone on the wide, wide sea of growing up.

LEARNING OPPORTUNITIES

- To explore issues connected to the world of adolescence (i.e., identity, alienation, peer relationships)
- To participate in strategies that help them understand those who are marginalized inside and outside the school community
- To make critical and thoughtful connections between experiences in fictional content and real-world situations
- To share personal stories and experiences in order to reflect on their own lives in relationship to others
- To use objects in symbolic and theatrical ways to understand the behaviors and emotions of a character
- To practice skills of using props and set to convey information to an audience
- To utilize the convention of still image/tableau in a variety of ways to represent themes and narratives connected to the idea of adolescence

- To develop skills of interpretation of text, scene building, and performance using single-line excerpts from scripts

Launching the Drama: Games that Focus on Identity

1. END OF THE LINE

- Arrange students in groups of five or six. Call out instructions for students to form a straight line, one behind the other, according to the following:
  - Shortest hair to longest hair
  - Alphabetical order (first name, last name)
  - Shoe sizes
  - Distance traveled to school
  - Street numbers

Extensions

Repeat any of the following instructions and challenge the students to line up in silence.

a) Each time a line is formed, the person who is at the front of the line instructs the person who is last in line to do an activity: e.g., three push ups, recite a nursery rhyme, sing a French song, etc.
b) After playing the game a few times, survey the group to find out who was at the front of the line the most number of times. Who was at the end of the line the most number of times?
c) Work as a whole class to play the line-up game. Students are paired off to discuss the following: What does the word "identity" mean to you? Pairs can then share their responses in groups of four, or with the whole class.

2. MIRROR, MIRROR

- Begin the activity by having students work in groups discussing the following: What kinds of things do people see when they look at themselves in the mirror (e.g., physical characteristics, clothing, age, gender)? Following the discussion, record student answers on a chart.
- The group is arranged in two lines facing each other. Each student is partnered with the person opposite them as A and B. To begin, the A partner tells the B partner five things they "see" when looking at him or her. The activity is reversed so that B partners tell five things they "see" when they look at A partners.
- All the B partners are instructed to shift one person to the right, so that each person has a new partner (the person at the end of the line moves to the front of the line). The game is repeated.
- The line shifts one more time so that new partners are formed. This time, partners in turn share five things about themselves that are NOT seen in the mirror, but are part of their identities; e.g., being a son, a guitar player, an employee, an immigrant, etc.

Extensions

a) Students move into groups of four. Students discuss

- What are some "in the mirror" things that we have in common?
- What are some invisible identities that we share?
- What is unique about my identity?

b) Students discuss the following lyrics by sharing answers to the questions in the two lines. Ask: How are the things we put in a résumé part of our identities?

> Who am I, anyway?
> Am I my résumé?
> —from the musical *A Chorus Line* by Marvin Hamlisch, Edward Kleban

3. TELL ME A STORY

- Students are arranged in an inner and outer circle arrangement so that each student has a partner.
- The students will tell thirty-second stories to each other in response to a number of teacher prompts.
- On a signal, the inner circle moves one to the right and the outer circle remains stationary. In this way students will be paired up with different partners.
- The activity continues through a variety of prompts (perhaps until students return to their original partner):

> Tell a story about yourself as: an adventurer, a traveler, a dreamer, a member of a family, a leader, a friend, a shopper, a winner, an artist, an environmentalist, etc.

4. *I AM...* MONOLOGUE

- Students are given a file card. Each student completes the following sentence stems to describe themselves:

> I was born…
> I care about…
> I am…

- The group stands in a circle. Each student in turn reads aloud the three items.
- The activity is repeated, the students choosing one item from the list that they think makes them unique. This can be written on the back of the card. Each person in turn, reads aloud the one sentence. Students read aloud their sentences.
- Students are arranged in groups of six or seven to create a group *I am...* monologue. Students can consider the following:

  - In what order will they present the lines?
  - What action, gesture will they use to accompany the line?
  - What tableau image can each person contribute to the presentation as he or she says a line?
  - What lines will be said solo? In pairs? As a group?
  - How will they begin and end their group monologue?

I am five six inches tall.
I weigh 150 pounds.
I have two arms.
Two legs
Two feet
Two ears
Two eyes
One nose
One mouth
Ten fingers
Ten toes.
I can taste.
I can smell.
I can see.
I can hear.
I can touch.
My blood is red.
My blood is red.
My blood is red.
My blood is red.
I breathe.
I think.
I feel.
I feel.
I feel.
I feel.
— from *Skin* by Dennis Foon

Extension

Students can write their own *I am...* poem using a number of sentence stems: e.g., *I am..., I feel..., I have..., I want..., I care about..., I like..., I hope...*

Framing the Theme: Focus on Identity

YESTERDAY, TODAY, AND TOMORROW: CREATING STILL IMAGES

Invite the class to brainstorm the stages of a person's life and agree on four significant stages: i.e., childhood, adolescence, adulthood, old age. Working in groups of four or five, students create a series of tableaux to show the life cycle of a person. Each still image should depict the essence of that stage of life. To prepare for this activity, students should consider the universal images that would represent that stage.

Ways to rehearse a series of tableaux:

- Review the elements of tableau and invite students to consider the elements in each of the tableaux
- Invite students to choose a director for each scene who will step out of the image to look as the audience and consider the elements of the tableaux
- Add a selection of music and ask students to allow the music to inform the way they move from one image to the next; i.e., transitions
- Ask students to go through the series forward, and then backward from the end to the beginning
- Ask students to find a personal focus for each of their positions in each of the scenes
- Encourage use of a prop or costume piece that is transformed from scene to scene

Ever stare at yourself so hard that your eyes practically start bleeding. I do.
—from *I, Claudia* by Kristen Thomson

Students can share their series of tableaux with the class. Invite students to share the sequence with two groups presenting at once. In order to accommodate the audience, invite the groups to run the sequence twice through. Two groups presenting at once will challenge the audience to observe both groups, and will give the groups a purpose for presenting the piece twice. Ask the audience to notice the similarities and differences in the work.

This activity is an opportunity for students to consider transitions. A transition is the movement from one image to the next. The movement from one tableau to the next should be smooth, economical (only what is necessary), and informed by the role the student is playing. Students should be encouraged to dissolve from one image and move in a way that depicts the character they are becoming in the next image.

Following the presentations, ask the audience:

- Which image do you think most effectively created the particular life stage?
- How did the groups use the prop to enrich our understanding of the particular life stage?
- What was similar in the baby pictures? Adolescent pictures?
- Which tableaux did you find easiest to create? Most challenging?
- What image stands out in your mind?
- Which image touched you personally and why?
- What does the sequence tell you about life?

Written Reflection

Invite students to respond to the following prompts to reflect on the sequence:

I felt most comfortable in the image of _____ because _____
_____.

The image of _____ reminded me of _____.

Watching the tableaux made me think of _____.

THE PLACE IN-BETWEEN: CAROUSEL PRESENTATIONS

Invite students to revisit and focus on the images of childhood and adolescence. Students consider an image that would exist between the two stages, the moment just before adolescence, and create the image in a tableau. Once they have prepared their images, they can be shared collectively in a circle using the Carousel method of presentation. Each group, in turn, presents his or her scene. The addition of music to accompany each scene will enhance the work.

Extension

Students repeat the activity by showing two images, the "in-between" time and the adolescent stage.

Reflection

Students discuss the following:

- What name might we give to this "in-between" stage of life?
- How is this stage of life different from other stages?
- What stories do you remember about this time in your life?

MAP OF MY BEDROOM

Map of My Bedroom is a useful drama strategy that also can be used when exploring a character. Students can pretend that they are a character from a source and conduct a guided tour with someone who wants to learn about the character.

Students work in pairs. Invite students to remember a time when they were becoming a teenager. Students consider what their bedroom looked like at this time of their life. Perhaps the bedroom looks the same now, but maybe there are bits and pieces from childhood poking out from closets and corners. Each person in turn takes a partner on a tour of the bedroom he or she had when he or she was a young adolescent. Students move through the imagined space as if they were really touring the room, examining the furniture, objects, wall decorations, closets, etc. The person touring the room can ask questions about the colors on the wall, posters, music or books on the shelf.

Following the activity, each partner can share something about their partner that they did not know before visiting the room. What can we learn about someone from visiting his or her room? If you were a set designer, creating a teenager's room, based on the tour, what items would you need to have in the room?

Extension

An alternative to this activity is to create a sketch that maps out the bedroom. Partners can exchange illustrations. Each person can report what he or she learned by examining this bedroom map.

Strategy Scheme: Experiencing Tableaux/Still Images

Patrice Baldwin has written several excellent resources that provide teachers with an overview of drama conventions, the purposes connected to each convention, as well as sample units of work that demonstrate the application of these conventions. Titles include

School Improvement Through Drama: A creative, whole class, whole school approach (2009)

The Primary Drama Handbook (2008)

With Drama in Mind: Real learning in imagined world (2007)

BEFORE, DURING, AFTER

Still images depict a moment in time. Students can represent a story by creating images in different periods of time and presenting two or more still images sequentially. These scenes can be set moments apart, or days or years apart. This is a convenient way to retell the story events; e.g., using three to five images to represent the beginning, middle, climax, and ending of a story.

EXPANDING THE MOMENT

A single moment in time can be represented in a variety of ways, with students creating images in different settings, with different characters. On a more abstract level, students can represent the different thoughts or feelings a character might be feeling at one point in time.

BROUGHT TO LIFE

A tableau can be activated and "brought to life" by having students create movement that grows out of a still image. The moving images can be returned to a frozen moment in time; e.g., the same image or different from the original. Music can be used to accompany the movements.

WHAT ARE YOU THINKING?

Once a tableau is created, the participants can speak their thoughts out loud. To prepare for this, students are invited to think about what the character might be thinking, feeling, or questioning at the moment represented in the tableau. Thoughts are uttered out loud in turn, perhaps by pointing to the character or approaching him or her with a tap on the shoulder.

MAY I ASK YOU A QUESTION?

Tell students that the characters (or objects) they have become are going to be questioned by the audience. The teacher or students watching the scene can interview one or more characters; i.e., students who answer in role. This is an opportunity to convey a character's motives, thoughts, and feelings at a particular moment, as well as a chance to reveal some narrative explanations.

OPPOSITES ATTRACT

Students can create two tableaux to represent contrasting images. This might show the different feelings a character might be experiencing in a dilemma, a decision the character is facing, or the visible truth and hidden truth about a particular situation. Hopes and fears, dreams and nightmares, past and present are some contexts that can be used to create contrasting tableaux images.

SCULPTING THE TABLEAU

The students are asked to become human clay. One or more people are invited to become the sculptor(s) who physically sculpts the clay into a still image. For this trust activity, the clay cannot speak or understand language, but relies on a sculptor to create a physical position, facial expression, and attitude to convey. Creating a statue or monument provides a context for the sculpture exercise.

BECOMING A DIRECTOR

Similar to the sculpture activity, this activity involves a still image created by having one person give instructions to the players. For this activity the "human clay" responds to verbal directions given by a sculptor/director.

NARRATIVE CAPTIONS

Once tableau images are created, narrative captions, similar to those in graphic stories, can be spoken out loud. These can be spoken either by the image-makers or by observers who haven't been part of creating the tableau.

COPY CAT

Photographs, illustrations, paintings, or sculptures are useful sources for tableau creations. Students are challenged to precisely re-create a scene that exists. Some students may wish to represent inanimate objects. The activity can be repeated, having students exchange roles to create the tableau. The Copy Cat activity can also have groups imitating exactly a tableau that has been created by another group.

EYES CLOSED/EYES OPEN

This is another way to present a series of images. Instructions are given to the audience by one member of the group saying, "Open your eyes/Close your eyes." When the audience is not watching, the groups can move from image to image. The process is repeated until a sequence of images has been shared. With this activity, the audience does not witness the transitions

CAROUSEL

This is a convenient structure for having students present still image scenes that they have rehearsed. The groups are given a performance order. On a signal, the first group slowly grows into their still image together, holds the image (for five silent seconds), and then melts back down. Each group presents their image in the pre-decided order. Students are encouraged to remain still as others perform.

GUIDED TOUR

One person is assigned to narrate a guided tour of a tableau image. Students, in role, can explain what each of the physical representations mean. Audience members can ask questions of the tour guide.

HOW DO I FIT IN?

Members of a group create a still image. Once it is completed, one person, who has been isolated from the rehearsal process, is invited to fit into the scene by adding himself or herself into the picture; e.g., a bystander adds himself/herself to a bully-and-victim scene. The role that is introduced and the relationship that is established by this additional image can change the meaning of the original tableau.

CROSSOVER

Students are divided into two groups. Each group creates a large tableau scene. These scenes might represent contrasting images; e.g., war and peace, hopes and fears. Once each group has created the still image, they are challenged to study and duplicate the scene that has been created by the other group. Students return to original scenes. On a signal, students cross over the room to create the still image of the other group. Musical accompaniment will enhance the performance of the still image scenes.

Extension

Groups can cross over and return to their original tableau scene.

A Drama Structure Using a Novel Excerpt

AN ADOLESCENT PHOTO ALBUM: CREATING STILL IMAGES

It is in doing drama with girls where I have discovered the most powerful examples of emancipatory education. In drama we can begin nowhere else but from "ourselves" where the personal and the cultural have a place.

—from *Drama Education in the Lives of Girls: Imagining possibilities* by Kathleen Gallagher (2000)

This activity helped students to capture images of a day in the life of a young adolescent. To begin, students walked about the room in different ways, according to instructions called out by the teacher: e.g., casually, quickly, jogging, on tiptoe, etc.

When the teacher called out a number, students formed groups that corresponded with that number. The teacher provided a title of a picture, and students froze into an image that represented that scene. After each scene had been created, students continued to move about the room until another instruction was given.

SOLO: Waiting for the Bus
PAIRS: At the Lockers
THREE: The Basketball Game
FOUR: The Cafeteria
FIVE: The School Dance
WHOLE CLASS: The Weekend

Once students had prepared the six scenes, they were invited to recreate the tableaux as the teacher called out random titles. Students were asked to revisit a scene more than once.

I AM AN OUTCAST: READING TEXT OUT LOUD

> I am an outcast.
>
>   The kids behind me laugh so loud I know they're laughing at me. I can't help myself. I turn around. It's Rachel surrounded by a bunch of kids wearing clothes that most definitely did not come from the Eastside Mall. Rachel Bruin my ex-best friend. She stares at something above my left ear. Words climb up my throat. This was the girl who understood about my parents, who didn't make fun of my bedroom. My throat burns. I can't speak.
>
> —from the novel, *Speak* by Laurie Halse Anderson

This activity encouraged students to revisit the text several times to further discover new meanings by experimenting with voice. After reading the text independently, students read the excerpt out loud at their own pace as they walked about the room. When they had completed the text, students were asked to remain on the spot. Students were asked to read the text in the following ways: with anger; with fear; in a whisper.

As a final activity, students worked in groups of four, standing in a line, to read the text out loud. Each sentence was read by one person in turn. The activity was repeated, having students change positions in line.

Students were invited to choose one line of text from the novel excerpt: e.g., "I turn around"; "My throat burns."

THE OUTCAST: REVISITING THE TABLEAU

Students returned to the images created in the adolescent photo album activity (see page 39); i.e., The Cafeteria groupings. Students were instructed to recreate the still images that depicted The Cafeteria scene. This time, students were asked to reshape the image by placing an outcast into the picture. This activity can be repeated by having the students revisit any of the scenes they created in An Adolescent Photo Album.

Students were asked to consider the thoughts of the people in the scene. The teacher tapped each student on the shoulder and invited them to provide one sentence or question that would suggest the inner thoughts of his or her character; e.g., *Why are they doing this to me? I hate to be hated*, etc. Students could also incorporate the lines from the excerpt into the tableaux.

Students shared the re-worked scenes.

Reflection

Students continued the discussion of the outcast with the following questions:

- How did the group choose to represent the Outcast physically?
- What does the tableau tell you about the Outcast that you did not know before?
- How did the tableaux make you feel about the Outcast?

THE OUTCAST'S STORY: HOT-SEATING

The class discussed the story by considering the following questions: How could we find out more about the Outcast? Who might we speak to? The students negotiated an age and name for her. In our drama, we called her Sarah.

Students brainstormed questions they wanted to ask about the Outcast. Students then considered who might be able to answer these questions: i.e., a family member, a guidance counselor, a neighbor she babysits for, etc. Using the convention of hot-seating, four characters from the list were selected to be interviewed or hot-seated and four students volunteered to play the roles.

Students selected which of the four characters they wanted to question first, and arranged their chairs in a circle around that character. After a few minutes, the teacher signaled the students to move to a different character, and then a third character, to interview.

Following the hot-seating, the teacher asked the students to share what they had learned from the characters. The teacher asked:

- What did we learn about Sarah?
- How did the characters in the hot seat feel about Sarah?
- If you were her, who would you trust?
- Can you believe these characters? Do you think they were withholding anything? Why?
- Did you learn anything about how Sarah became an outcast?
- Do you have any theories as to how this happened?

CREATING SARAH'S BEDROOM: DEFINING SPACE

In order to learn more about Sarah, her story and feelings, the students created her bedroom, a space that was important to her in her life. The teacher brought in a knapsack of objects belonging to Sarah and emptied the knapsack on the floor in front of the students. The students observed the objects—random objects, such as a teddy bear, music box, photograph of teenagers, etc.—and were asked to bring other objects to the circle that they thought might have belonged to Sarah. Students brought objects, including personal items such as keys, jewelry, notebooks, MP3 players, and cell phones, from their own purses and knapsacks, as well as collecting objects from the room.

In silence, the students used the available furniture in the room and the collected objects to create Sarah's bedroom. As the activity continued, students negotiated the placement of objects, continually moving items. At a cue from the teacher they stepped back, were invited to make a few more changes if they felt they were needed, and then more or less came to consensus.

BUILDING SARAH'S LIFE: OBJECTS OF CHARACTER

Having built Sarah's room, the students were asked to imagine that the room they built was the set for the play. They were invited to walk through and respectfully explore the set, but not move any items. They explored the set in silence, closely examined the objects in the room, and then stood beside an object that they were drawn to for any reason. Students created the stories of these objects, in groups if more than one person had moved to the same object, or alone. They considered: who might have given the object to Sarah; how and why it was given to her; how she might feel about it now; why she has it in this place. Upon creating the stories of the objects, the students negotiated who Sarah would take through her room on a tour and share the significance of the objects with. The students decided that Sarah would take a neighbor who had just moved into the neighborhood, and who would therefore not know Sarah's story. It was decided that the neighbor was slightly older than Sarah.

The teacher could model hot-seating by first playing one of the roles and inviting the whole class to interview her. The teacher should also instruct students to keep the drama open when they are in the hot seat, using the information from the exploration of the text and imagining what that character might know and be willing to share. Students can also choose not to answer a question in role if it is too personal or they do not know the answer.

Well, I had some very private objects in my room that isn't stuff I want to give away and isn't stuff that my mom is allowed to comb through. Like, there were things hidden underneath by bed. Like Evidence and secret objects and personal musings. Like, essentially the whole stock of my private emotional life…

—from *I, Claudia* by Kristen Thomson

… I wanted to give you something all the same. You see, I have spent my life running from my past and yet I have carried fragments of it around in this old suitcase. And I don't know if these things will make much sense to you… they hardly make sense to me but it's all I have to give you.

—from the play *When the Rain Stops Falling* by Andrew Bovell

I am the mirror where his squalid
    reflection
He, shaving, subjects to indifferent
    inspection.
Morning by morning I see that
    face,
Dustily returning its gaze.
—from the play *The Habit of Art* by
Alan Bennett

REVEALING SARAH'S STORIES: STORYTELLING AS THE OBJECT

One student played the role of Sarah and one student played the neighbor, and together they entered the room. The rest of the students stood around, creating the walls of the room. Sarah and the neighbor slowly moved through the room and, when they picked up or stood beside an object a student had developed a story for, that student told the story in the role of the object. For example: *I am Sarah's bracelet and I was given to her by her mom.* In this way, Sarah's story was built and revealed collectively.

Following the tour, the students stepped out of role and out of the set, and discussed the new information they learned about Sarah through visiting her bedroom and learning about the objects in her life.

An alternative for this activity is to ask students to bring in an item that they think would reveal something about the character. These could be placed in the knapsack one-by-one or set about the character's room.

IF I WERE YOU...: SHARING AND REFLECTING

One student volunteered to assume the role of the Outcast, Sarah. The group was invited to place the Outcast somewhere in her bedroom: e.g., on her bed, sprawled out on her desk, sitting in a corner, etc. Students went into the set and physically molded Sarah in the space. Several negotiated choices were made before a final image was decided upon.

As a reflective activity, students were asked to give advice to the Outcast given what they now know about her life. Students approached the Outcast one by one, sometimes making a physical connection, placing a hand on her shoulder. As each student came forward, she or he completed the line, "If I were you..."

Students then discussed what they thought the future of the Outcast's life might be, how might she best carry forward. How could she become part of the group again?

LOOKING FORWARD: DEVELOPING THEORIES

The teacher and students discussed and recapped the information gathered through the hot-seating and through creating and visiting Sarah's room. Using this information, students developed theories about what may have contributed to Sarah's separation from the group, how she became the Outcast: Why was she alienated from the group? Was it one particular event or a series of events that led her best friend to turn against her?

Following the discussion, each group chose one word to express the essence of the theory and one word to express how to begin to resolve the situation, a first step in bringing Sarah back to the group. The students created two images with a transition to communicate the words, and inserted the words into the images, either inside the images or as transitions. The students shared the images and words in a circle, moving seamlessly from one group to the other.

Students looked for similarities in the theories and together agreed on one particular theory, pulling together some of the ideas from each of the groups. This was not difficult, because students had collectively built the information in the previous two activities.

Two chairs were placed on the playing area and two students volunteered to play Sarah and the best friend, representing the voice of the group that has alienated Sarah. The rest of the students formed a circle around the players and decided where and how to place the characters in the scene. Students placed their chairs in relation to the characters, deciding if they wanted to speak for the best friend as part of a collective voice or to speak for Sarah as part of a collective voice.

The students improvised the conversation between the two young women. The teacher facilitated encouraging students to speak one at a time, listening and responding to each other. Students were instructed that they could move their chairs and positions at any time if they wanted to speak for the other character. Students did move their chairs and experience both perspectives.

The teacher brought the work to a close when she felt that the students had come to some kind of consensus and had made progress in bringing the Outcast back to the group. They agreed on a closing line for the scene and a closing position for the characters.

Reflection

The students discussed the activity of creating collective roles and the way the scene ended. The students considered the following questions in their discussion:

- Do you think the scene ended realistically, authentically?
- Will Sarah be able to move forward with her friends?
- What have we learned about relationships and communication in this drama?
- How important is it to feel that you belong?
- How is our identity shaped and influenced by our friends and peer groups?
- What have you learned about yourself through this drama?
- What have you learned about outcasts in the world?

Who Am I? Creating Images of Self

by Sheena Robertson, freelance arts educator

As a teacher and artist-educator in inner city Toronto, something that has always struck me as most unjust are the negative images created by members of the media who live *outside* the communities, to depict the young people who live *in* them. There is an image which I see over and over again—taken by many different photographers, but communicating the same stereotype. You've seen it too: *Two young black men, wearing baggy clothes, hats turned backwards, chains around their necks, arms crossed scowling down at the camera, which is taking the photo from a low angle.*

This image was always jarring to me, because it didn't reflect what I knew to be true about the amazing and complex young people around me. I had the opportunity to work with arts project with Inner City teenagers. In the initial session, they were provided with a range of photographic images that help us consider representation and stereotyping:

- How can the truth of a culture be captured in single images?
- Who is being represented in these images? Who isn't?

We then started a photographic journey of our own—where students could learn about photographic literacy and create images of how *they* wanted to represent themselves and their community.

The project centred on the photographic elements of design. Students examined a number of photo images from magazines to consider the use of light; composition, the rule of thirds; the use of color, line, shape, texture, visual balance, and pathways; and a variety of shot types. Students then worked in groups and each was assigned a different shot type or angle to consider: i.e., *extreme close up, close up, medium shot, long shot, wide shot, high angle, low angle.* A range of samples was offered to each group and the students chose a favorite photo that best represented their category. Using a number of digital cameras, the students created images of the self: *How, through photography, do I/can I present the truth of who I am to others?*

As students participated in these explorations, they were creating photographic images intended to express to people outside of their communities *who they are* (in all their complexities). They were invited to create images that were abstract or literal, metaphoric or symbolic. Students were asked to be selective—professional photographers will often take 100 photos for every one that is published. If students were reluctant writers, we had them record audio records for each photo selected.

As a culminating activity, we created an exhibit of large printed 16" x 20" photographs accompanied by an audio recording of fragments of the students' writing, overlapping to create an audio symphony of their voices. A less-expensive sharing would be to project images from a digital projector while students perform a choral-speaking or spoken-word piece about themselves or their community.

Photographing images takes the students beyond the world of tableaux. In drama class we often ask students to freeze into images to represent a theme, idea, or concept. Taking photographs helped students to extend their understanding of representing images physically and, as this project demonstrates, promoted a critical understanding of conveying, through an art form, the truth of *Who I Am.*

Extending the Drama

WRITING IN ROLE: TEXT MESSAGE

Students can write a text message conversation between the Outcast and a friend who still supports the Outcast. As part of the conversation, ask the students to consider advice the friend might offer.

IMPROVISATION: A YEAR IN THE LIFE OF AN OUTCAST

The class can be arranged into four groups. Each group improvises a scene that would represent a significant episode in the Outcast's life. Using cues from the novel excerpt, students prepare scenes that would tell a story about the Outcast at different periods of time. The following captions might serve as prompts for the improvisations:

a) An argument with her best friend: How did they become ex-friends?
b) Shopping at the Mall: Why is she being outcast?
c) Meeting the parents: What can we learn about her parents?
d) I can't speak: Why does the Outcast refuse to speak?

DREAMS OF THE PAST AND FUTURE: DANCE DRAMA

Invite students to create a sequence of four or five tableaux with transitions that would reveal a dream the Outcast might have had. This dream could express how she became an outcast, or it could reveal her future. What might she hope for? What might she be afraid of? Who might become important in her life? Students present these dreams using musical accompaniment. The class can discuss the various interpretations that were depicted.

I AM AN OUTCAST, CONT'D: WRITING A MONOLOGUE

Students can add to the Outcast monologue by adding to the novel excerpt. Using information from the drama, students write in role as the Outcast, telling a story or expressing her feelings.

A POSTER ON THE WALL: CREATING A COLLAGE

Students can use a variety of media to create a collage that might appear in the Outcast's bedroom. What magazine photos might they include? What words or phrases from newspapers or magazines would be featured in this poster? Students can also create a collage with digital images and music.

SARAH'S PLAYLIST

Invite students to create Sarah's playlist. They can select the song she is listening to most often right now and explain why she chooses this song.

IDENTITY MASK

Students created masks to represent their identities. They considered

- What colors should the mask feature?
- What designs, shapes, or symbols should be used to represent their identities?

Mask and Character Development
by Teodoro Dragonieri, educator, artist

A mask tells us more than a face.
—Oscar Wilde

There are three masks: The one we think we are, the one we really are and the one we have in common.
—Jacques Lecoq

The power of the mask in education, therapy, and theatre is exceptional. Few inanimate objects are as universally successful in riveting attention, stimulating the imagination, and arousing deep emotions. The use of the mask as an element of theatre, of storytelling, and of carnivalesque transformation is wide-spread. The mask facilitates the exploration of characterization and engenders broader physicality. The mask gives depth and meaning to gestures, procures a voice for itself and its wearer, reminds us of the importance of silence and stillness. It influences the creation of complete, fully dimensional characters while discovering creativity, enriching intuition, encouraging risk-taking, and joyfully developing the inner clown.

When students are invited to explore masks, they are engaged in a discovery process, utilizing their bodies and voices, that draws upon their emotions, perceptions, experiences, and memories. The goal in introducing such work is to elicit immediate, intuitive, and instinctual responses to both mask and character. At the core of my work is a personal belief that *I am in all the masks and all the masks are in me.*

Working with masks is a challenging process: I don't begin with masks at all. Much of the early exploratory work is done with eyes closed or with a blindfold, so the students do not feel self-conscious. The exercises are done quickly and without a great deal of thinking to strengthen the participants' trust in their own intuition, to allow for risk-taking, and to eradicate the "critic" within.

Exploration Exercises

1. Being Neutral

- Stand in a circle and assume the "neutral" body position (one devoid of distinguishing characteristics/qualities).
- Establish rhythmical breathing; i.e., breathe in for three seconds, hold your breath for three seconds, and exhale for the same count.
- Draw on your memory and select a character from your life experiences. The character could be someone you know well, or a chance encounter.
- At the count of ten, starting from a neutral position, assume the physical attributes of the character. Act immediately, without thinking too much.

2. Adding Voice

Once you have established the physical persona, you will learn to breathe in character. The breathing will vary according to various factors like age, energy, emotional state, health, and posture. To develop the voice, do the following exercises (each are about one minute in duration): after each step, when asked, share.

- Create sounds/noises that your character would make.
- Choose a vowel that best connects to the spirit of your character. Create as many sound variations as you can. Experiment with volume, tempo, and rhythm.
- Repeat the preceding step, with one word.
- Repeat the preceding step, now with a full sentence.
- For a few minutes, in character, interact with others and enjoy the wonderful array of entities created.

3. Hello, Mask!

- In silence, choose one of the half masks provided.
- Sit on the floor and place the mask directly in front of you. Using the floor as support for the mask, close your eyes and feel the contours of the mask by rubbing your hands all over it. Rub, in isolation, individual features of the mask: i.e., the eyes, the upper mouth area, the nose.
- Proceed to sculpt the physical attributes of the mask to your face as if it were a chunk of clay. Hold the expression you have sculpted on your face. Open your eyes and place the actual mask on your face.
- Looking into the mirror provided, see if you have embodied the physical features of the mask. Ensure that a connection is made between the mask and the rest of your face.
- Wearing the mask, repeat all steps in exercise 2. Adding Voice.

4. Shaping Character

To refine your characterization and end up with a "body memory" of your masked character, do the following:

- Stand in a circle and turn to the outside.
- For ten seconds, assume your character's physicality.
- Turn to the inside of the circle and reveal.
- Repeat these three steps, changing the count: from ten seconds, to five, to three, and finally at the sound of a clap.
- Enjoy seeing and feeling the transformation that occurs. Engage your fellow masked characters. For a few minutes admire the mask characters that come alive physically and vocally.

Core Principles of Mask Movement

Reveal

- The aim of the mask is both to reveal and to hide: you hide your face but you reveal your body. A "reveal" should last a minimum of three seconds.
- Revealing or presenting your mask character, by facing the audience and pausing, should occur every time you enter and exit.

Be Still

- Entrances and exits must be punctuated with a moment of stillness.
- Stillness should present specific aspects of the character, adding depth to the performance.

Report to the Audience
- Plot is character in action: periodic speech to the audience engages them in your story.
- Share each idea, every thought and discovery, by communicating directly with the audience. Make contact. Look at and confide in those who are witnessing the action.

Shape the Body to the Mask

Physicality keeps the mask alive. Without the support of the physicality, the mask and the character do not live.\

Embrace the Alternate or Opposite Feelings
- Portray, at times, the opposite of what the mask displays, by changing your physicality.
- The mask, by itself, does not determine the emotions that can be expressed: a happy mask can become sad by simply changing the deportment of the body.

Script Variation: Fragments from Canadian Plays

INTERPRETING SCRIPT FRAGMENTS

See page 50 for a list of script fragments.

Sources

White Biting Dog by Judith Thomson
Tough by George F. Walker
Better Living by George F. Walker
The Shape of a Girl by Joan MacLeod
Still Stands the House by Gwen Pharis Ringwood
The Ecstasy of Rita Joe by George Ryga
Leaving Home by David French
What Glorious Times They Had by Diane Grant
Dry Lips Oughta Move to Kapuskasing by Tomson Highway
Liars by Dennis Foon
Les Belles Soeurs by Michel Tremblay

Provide students with the page of lines of dialogue, and ask them to approach the lines like a script. The following outline has students interpret these fragments independently:

- Students read through the lines silently.
- Students choose any line to begin with and read through the lines out loud. Once they reach the bottom of the list, they begin to read from the top of the list. In this way, students will not be reading the lines in unison.
- Students choose a new line to begin reading. This time, students walk around the room as they read lines aloud.
- Students read several times through the lines in a variety of ways; e.g., changing tempo, changing volume.
- Students select a line that intrigued them and memorize the selected line.
- Students form groups of three and share their lines with others. The activity is repeated, with students saying the lines as a greeting, as if it were an amazing story, as a compliment, as an insult, as a very funny joke, etc.
- Students meet up with a partner. On a signal, each person begins to recite his or her line. The students improvise a conversation that grows from the two lines.

DELIVERING THE LINES AND IMPROVISING A SCENE

- Students in pairs are arranged in two rows, A and B, with partners facing each other. A is invited to begin by reciting one of the lines. B responds to A by improvising dialogue. The pairs improvise a brief scene.
- The activity is repeated with students in row B delivering the opening lines and students in row A responding, as together they improvise a scene.
- Students in row A are instructed to move down the line to the left so that each A faces a new partner. The activity is repeated.
- Students continue to encounter new partners by moving down the line. Students are assigned different ways to consider the delivery of their lines: e.g. beginning with a handshake, using a strong emotion, as if said by the boss of a company, reducing the line to one word, etc.

Extension

Students perform on the spot to show moments of their scenes with a cue from the teacher. Students have an opportunity to observe the multiple meanings in the words and the variety of interpretations of a single line.

INTERPRETING AND MAKING MEANING

Working with a partner, students create scenes using only their two lines. To prepare for this improvisation, students need to consider the order in which the lines will be introduced, the setting of the scene, the relationship between the characters.

Once they have rehearsed, students share their mini scenes with another pair. In observing the scenes, students are asked to notice the interpretation of the lines and the relationship of the characters. How did the students communicate the relationship, the setting, with only these two lines?

The students then create new groups of four and number themselves 1 to 4. Each group is given a chair to place in the middle of the group. In the order of the numbers, students move to the chair and deliver their lines, attempting as much as possible to connect with the previous lines. Following the scenes, the students discuss the connection of the lines, which lines said one after the other made sense, and which lines would make more sense delivered in a different order. Students create scenes altering the order, deciding on entrances and exits, on their delivery of the lines, on their movement and physical positions. Groups rehearse and share their scenes. The audience is asked to observe and consider:

- What choices did the students make in creating the scene?
- Did anyone in the scene deliver your line? How did their interpretation differ from yours?
- Did the actors convey "truth" to the scenes?
- In a word or two, what is the scene really about? How do you know this?

BACK TO THE SCRIPT: BUILDING A SCRIPT ON ADOLESCENCE

Working in groups of four or five, students return to the one-liners and select any eight to ten lines to create a scene, focusing on either the Adolescent Journey or Sarah's Journey from the Outcast drama. The students are challenged to use only the assigned lines and cannot include improvised dialogue. In building a truthful scene, they decide on a context, create a working set, and discuss the relationship between the characters. Students rehearse and share their scenes, introducing each scene with a title.

Reflection

Following the presentations the students discuss:

- Apart from the context of adolescence, did you notice any recurring themes in the presentations?
- What did you especially like about each of the scenes?
- Which scene do you think connected closely with your scene?
- Could we put these scenes into an order to create an anthology? How would you order the scenes?
- What have you learned about interpretation from this scene work?

Extensions

a) Students can continue to develop a monologue from one of their lines to further deepen their understanding of a character.

b) In groups, students can improvise the scene that might happen before or after the created script.

c) Invite students to remember and record lines of dialogue that they overhear in their daily life and have them, in groups of three, create a new scene with overheard lines.

Script Fragments

There are more important things in life than going out with cute guys.

I like him but how am I supposed to feel comfortable around him…

So this is where you've been hiding out, eh?

You gonna do this? You gonna believe her?

Fly to the moon…that's what I'd like to do…or maybe Mars…or maybe just float in the endless vacuum of space.

There's only one way I am coming home and it is this way…

I'll be with you. It won't happen with me there.

You never think about it because then you realize you could lose it, it could be taken away.

Yea, I got totally wasted and fell… on my lip.

Oh I think she does. You haven't seen them. I mean they're like all over each other in there.

So I know some things about you, some things you don't know, like how you feel.

Oh I did bigger things too…well I never used it to save a human life but…a couple of times…

Sorry I screwed up again. I don't seem to fit in anywhere, do I?

And you come up to the kitchen and you plunk yourself down like you owned the place.

Sometimes, just sometimes I dream about him. I dream…

I feel like …I don't know…I'm just out there, really out there.

Wanting is tomorrow's stuff and until it happens it's not real.

Now if you've got something to say to me, say it.

I like arguing with you. You argue like a guy.

Do I look scared? Do you think I am afraid of you?

I knew it! I knew I'd do something more special than work in a mall.

We did a good job. Even Sophie hates Sophie.

I never cry. I sometimes get very scared but I never cry.

There's no mistakin' where you've been to and it's not to church.

Everything and anything I ever said about life or what I wanted in life you agreed with.

She can't take care of herself, let alone us.

You want to know how hard it is to raise a kid on your own?

This is not something you can hide. Your whole idiot face is an open book.

Pembroke Publishers ©2010 *Drama Schemes, Themes & Dreams* by Larry Swartz and Debbie Nyman ISBN 978-1-55138-253-1

Assessment: Tableaux Checklist

Name: _____ Date: _____

Excellent

_____ Focal point is very clearly established; i.e., communicating idea, event, or story
_____ Highly effective use of space in the arrangement of the image
_____ Use of varying levels adds strong impact to the depiction
_____ Strong facial expressions and gesture that contribute meaning and add power
_____ All players are in clear view of the audience
_____ Transitions are extremely smooth and add dramatic effect to the presentation
_____ Evidence of thorough organization and rehearsal to create image collaboratively

Very Good

_____ Focal point is clearly established; i.e., communicating idea, event, or story
_____ Effective use of space in the arrangement of the image
_____ Use of varying levels adds impact to the depiction
_____ Effective use of facial expressions and gesture that contribute meaning and add power
_____ Most players are in clear view of the audience
_____ Transitions are smooth and add dramatic effect to the presentation
_____ Evidence of good organization and rehearsal to create image collaboratively

Good

_____ Focal point is appropriately established; i.e., communicating idea, event, or story
_____ Good use of space in the arrangement of the image
_____ Good use of varying levels adds impact to the depiction
_____ Good use of facial expressions and gesture that contribute meaning and add power
_____ Few players are in clear view of the audience
_____ Transitions add some dramatic effect to the presentation
_____ Evidence of some organization and planning to create image collaboratively

Not Yet

_____ Focal point needs to be established; i.e., communicating idea, event, or story
_____ Need to consider use of space in the arrangement of the image
_____ Limited use of varying levels adds impact to the depiction
_____ Limited use of facial expressions and gesture that contribute meaning and add power
_____ All participants need to be aware of audience in presenting the image
_____ Transitions add limited dramatic effect to the presentation
_____ Evidence of minimal organization and rehearsal to create image collaboratively

Pembroke Publishers ©2010 *Drama Schemes, Themes & Dreams* by Larry Swartz and Debbie Nyman ISBN 978-1-55138-253-1

The Bully Dance

The Theatre of Urban: Youth and schooling in dangerous times by Kathleen Gallagher presents an in-depth ethnographic study that evokes the challenges and rewards of the urban drama classroom.

Too much time in schools is spent on how to "manage" conflict and on punitive modes of address; tomes have been written on the subject of "bullying." Governments the world over continue to spend millions on "comprehensively anti-bullying plans." My own view is that there is much to be gained from a creative exploration of conflict, the very kind that routinely interrupts the functioning of most high school classrooms.
— From *The Theatre of Urban: Youth and schooling in dangerous times* by Kathleen Gallagher (2007: 140)

Drama Theme: Bullying

The statistics are irrefutable. The headlines are frightening. The stories are painful. Bullying has always been—and continues to be—a challenging issue in classrooms, in communities, and in society. To prepare students to grow as caring citizens of the world, it is important that teachers help students to identify, understand, and confront problems with bullying in all its hostile forms. What procedures, policies, and programs are in place to acknowledge and address bullying? How do we help young people live with integrity, civility, and compassion?

If we are to raise kids who can think and act ethically, we don't begin with the thinking or the acting. We begin with caring.
— from *Just because it's not wrong, doesn't make it right* by Barbara Coloroso (2005)

In her book, *The Bully, The Bullied and The Bystander*, Barbara Coloroso defines bullying as "a conscious, willful, and deliberate hostile activity intended to harm, induce fear through the threat of further aggression, and create terror" (2002: 13). Working inside and outside poems, scripts, and stories that feature bullies and their targets enables students to empathize and to see alternative ways of behaving and responding. Through drama work, they will have an opportunity to explore the complexities of trusting, negotiating, problem-solving, cooperating, and living with others. By creating and exploring the identities and dilemmas of fictional characters seeking a safe place to belong, students can come to a better understanding of the relationships in their own lives. It matters.

LEARNING OPPORTUNITIES

- To provide an open forum for discussion and analysis of the bully, the bullied, and the bystander
- To provide a context for students to express their feelings and experiences of bullying
- To help students understand why students bully and how they may stop

- To build understanding of a target's perspective by taking a role that promotes empathy
- To consider strategies for dealing more effectively with bullies
- To help students make connections to bullying issues by responding to script, poetry, and novel excerpts
- To explore techniques for rehearsing and presenting choral dramatization with poetry
- To engage actively in drama exploration and role play with a focus on examining issues and themes in poetry

Launching the Drama: Circle Games to Build Inclusion

1. THAT'S ME!

- This game can be played with students sitting at their desks, or randomly about the room. They might sit in chairs in a circle so they can notice one another.
- The leader calls out different instructions and players stand and shout out "That's me!" if it applies to them. As students stand, they are encouraged to notice others they have something in common with.
- An alternative way to play this game is to have students stand in a circle and step forward if an item applies to them.

Stand if…
- You were born in the summer.
- You have a brother.
- You are wearing glasses.
- You have won a prize.
- You can play a musical instrument.
- You bought something new to wear this month.
- You have read all of the Harry Potter novels.
- You have been to Disneyworld.
- You own a dog.
Etc.

Extensions

a) As students become familiar with the game, additional topics might be added that would reveal issues connected to their identity and culture. Note: As the game continues, some issues may be sensitive for the participants. Always give them the choice of standing/stepping forward or not.

Stand if…
- You were born in this country.
- Both your parents work.
- You can speak more than two languages.
- You have a job.
- At least one of your grandparents immigrated to this country.
- You like the name you were born with.
Etc.

b) Instead of a leader calling out items, students can volunteer to suggest things that they might have in common with others.

2. BLOWING IN THE WIND

- Students stand in a circle with one player standing in the centre. That person is It and says "The wind blows for anyone who…" and calls out a description that applies to himself or herself: e.g., "The wind blows for anyone wearing blue jeans"; "The wind blows for anyone who was born in August"; etc.
- Students that the description applies to must move, and exchange places with another student matching the description. The person who is It tries to take a place in the circle.
- The last player without a place in the circle becomes It, and calls out another item that "blows in the wind."

3. BUNNY! BUNNY! BUNNY!

To prepare for this game, students imitate the leader step-by-step in the following ways:

- Leader becomes a bunny, by putting hands on either side of head as "bunny ears" and wiggling fingers.
- Leader repeats the above activity, this time saying the word "Bunny" as actions are performed. The word "Bunny" is said in a variety of voices.
- The group stands in a circle.
- The person on the leader's right becomes the right ear of the bunny by making a right "bunny ear"; the person on the left becomes the left ear of the bunny by making a left "bunny ear."
- The leader begins to perform bunny movements in the centre of the circle. Encourage the leader to move in different ways, to use different voices, and to use a variety of levels.
- The challenge is for the "bunny ears" to imitate exactly what the bunny is doing.
- The leader can decide at any time to choose a new bunny leader by standing in front of a person in the circle. A new bunny trio is formed and the game continues. The previous leader and the "ears" take a space back in the circle.

4. KUMBA, KUMBA…

- The group stands in a circle. A rhythmic clapping beat is established by the leader. The leader calls out the words "Kumba, Kumba…" and the group joins in.
- Once the group is comfortable with the rhythm, an action is introduced. The leader makes a puppet-like movement snapping in rhythm, first to his face, then to any other player in the circle:

  "Monkey, Monkey" (snapping toward own face)
  "Monkey, Monkey" (choosing a new person in the circle)

- That person, in turn, repeats the "Monkey, Monkey" action (snapping toward own face, then choosing a new person in the circle).

- The group continues to say "Kumba, Kumba, Kumba…" in rhythm.
- A new gesture is then introduced. If someone is a "Monkey," the players on either side say "Tonka, Tonka"; they face each other and make a mirror movement, going side-by-side with arms and legs swinging.
- The game continues with new gestures being introduced until everyone is involved.

5. CIRCLE TAG

- Students work in groups of four or five; each group forms a circle.
- One person is designated to be the Target, and one is designated to remain outside the circle as It.
- The challenge is for It to tag the Target. The participants in the circle have the task of protecting the Target.
- Once the Target is tagged, new players are chosen as Target and It.
- Following the game, students can discuss how the game represents real-life situations (e.g. bullying).

6. CHAOS

- Sitting in circle with a student in the middle, students make eye contact with each other to communicate that they agree to switch places. While students are changing places, the student in the middle tries to slip into a seat.
- The person in the middle can call "Chaos!" at any time, and then everyone has to change chairs.
- Encourage students not to simply move one place to the left or right, but instead to move farther across the circle.

You don't have to like every kid in school, but you have to honor their humanity.
— Barbara Coloroso, April 12, 2010

A Place for All: An Epiphany of Sorts
by Debra McLauchlan, drama professor, Brock University

In over a decade in the high-school drama classroom, I taught Grade 9 at least twenty times. A multitude of memories are attached to those years, many ranging over extended days and weeks as students grew in maturity and ability. No two classes were ever the same; no two students exactly alike. But whatever the class, there was always lots of activity; an abundance of energy; a host of problems to be solved; and a range of emotions, ideas, and stories to be expressed and shared. The specific memory I have chosen to write about involves a 14-year-old girl I will call Holly, a girl with a passion for drama, a fiery temper, and Down's syndrome.

The first two weeks of the Grade 9 course introduced students to various team-building and collaborative activities that became more and more drama-focused as the days progressed. The intention was for the class to gradually build a sense of shared identity in which students worked productively in pre-assigned groups with all of their peers. Through whole-class discussion, students identified behaviors that signaled both positive and negative group interaction. At the end of each class, I verbally summarized examples I had witnessed, without naming names or using judgmental language. By the end of two weeks, students were usually able to demonstrate a practical knowledge of effective teamwork strategies.

From the first day of the course, Holly was accompanied to class by an educational assistant (EA) who stayed with her assigned group until Holly grasped whatever task was involved in an activity. After a few minutes, the EA would discreetly move from within the group's space to an observer's position a comfortable distance away. Initially, the EA and I both noticed the veiled disregard a few students conveyed upon discovering that Holly was in their group. Many others accepted Holly's presence, but overtly discounted her ability to contribute anything truly positive, and treated her as a benign obstacle to their group's success. Holly mostly remained quiet during those first two weeks of class, but in the resource room released her anger and frustration. Although eager to express herself through drama, Holly felt silenced and invalidated by many of her classmates

One day, I purposely created a working group of students who had displayed a noticeable willingness to welcome Holly. The culminating task for the lesson was to create a "living" group statue to be displayed in a Museum of Human Emotions. In their assigned groups, students first selected an emotion or mood to illustrate, and then decided upon an event and setting that might elicit this state of mind. Next, they arranged various risers, platforms, and rostra to suggest distinctive features of the location or event. No objects or furniture were allowed. With a physical configuration in place, students assigned themselves characters to portray within the group statue. Following guidelines for creating tableaux, they posed themselves within the setting to portray the emotion or mood they had chosen. Students then decided on an order for their characters to create themselves from "lumps of clay."

The class practiced their presentation three times with classical music playing in the background. They all began with everyone situated as lumps of clay in their predetermined spaces. One by one, each group member slowly and fluidly evolved into his or her component of the group statue. The presentation ended in a final tableau of all characters in their respective positions. The class ended with groups presenting their work, and classmates offering suggestions about the emotion or mood, setting, and event portrayed.

Holly's group, portraying "hope," was the last to present. And, within her group, Holly's was the last character to move into position. Initially she was crouched as a lump of clay on a high central riser so that we saw her in full profile. Gradually, she raised herself to a kneeling posture on the hard wooden structure, then slowly lifted her upper body and brought her hands together in a prayer position. She then raised her arms aloft and tilted her face toward the ceiling, her long blond hair falling down her back. Her expression was mesmerizing. For what seemed like minutes, Holly remained absolutely frozen while the entire class drew an astonished breath of silence. The EA and I glanced at each other, but turned away quickly when we saw contagious tears in each other's eyes. We both felt strongly that we had witnessed Holly's soul in her performance.

That revealing moment, riveting and astonishing as it was, did not spark enduring change in some students' attitudes toward Holly. But it did earn her a measure of increased respect and acceptance. As weeks transpired and she became more comfortable in the environment, Holly grew more and more vocal and demanding. Sometimes she burst into angry outbursts of disagreement with her assigned working group. Sometimes she removed herself physically and sat sulking in a corner. Occasionally she refused to enter the classroom at all. But whenever her behavior challenged and exasperated me, I intentionally recalled the day when Holly's masterful prayer revealed the soulful core of her passion for drama.

Framing the Theme: The Bully, the Bullied, and the Bystander

THE BULLY: FROM STILL IMAGE TO IMPROVISATION

- Students create a statue entitled The Bully. Once each person has created a still image, draw their attention to the hand gestures represented in each statue. What is the message behind each of these gestures: e.g., arms folded, fists, pointed fingers?
- Students create a statue entitled The Victim. Once each person has created a still image, draw their attention to way the head has been placed. How are these images different than the bully image? What is the message behind each of these positions; e.g., hands in front of face, lowered head, scared look?
- Divide the class in half. Group #1 re-creates the bully statue, while Group #2 watches. What do they notice about the bully images?

- Group #2 then re-creates the victim/target statues while Group #1 watches. What do they notice about these images?
- Group #1 re-creates the bully statue one more time. Tell each person in Group #2 to match up with a bully to create a new tableau featuring two people.
- Invite each student to consider what the person he or she is portraying is thinking at that moment. Tap the shoulder of each participant to signal them to call out the thought of the character he or she has become. Tell students they might be called upon more than once. They can repeat a line or come up with a new line.
- Students re-create their tableaux images. This time they bring the scene to life. Each student can improvise conversation from his or her own character's point of view. The goal of this activity is to spontaneously respond to what each of the characters says. Note: It is important to remind students that the bully and the target are not allowed to touch each other at this point. Challenge the students to stay in role for one minute.
- On a signal, have students switch roles, so the bully becomes the target. Pairs can begin by recreating the still image. Students can use some of the conversation from the previous improvisation, but they are not required to repeat the exact same conversation. Challenge the students to stay in role for 90 seconds.
- Partners return to their original roles and repeat the improvisation. Advise students that you will not assign a time limit. Can the victim persuade the bully to stop the behavior? What arguments will he or she give?
- Have the targets stand in front of the bully characters. Interview them to determine what took place. Some questions might be:

> Why is this person picking on you?
> Do you think this bully targets other people?
> What was the most hurtful thing the bully said to you?
> What did you do/say to persuade the bully to stop?
> Do you think you could ever be friends with this person?
> Are you going to tell others about this incident?

Extensions

a) Students can work with their partners to create a new improvisation that might take place later that day or week. Those students who were the bully character become the target that they tormented. Those who were the target become someone who the target might turn to: e.g. a sibling, a best friend, an employer, a neighbor, a social worker, a police officer. The goal of this improvisation is

- to have the target tell his or her story
- to offer solutions about what might be done to deal with the bully

Following the improvisation, survey the students to find out what kind of advice (if any) was given to the target. The class can discuss strategies that a target might take to prepare for dealing with the bully.

b) Students can work in groups of three. One person is a bully, one is the bullied, and one is the bystander. The bystander is an eyewitness to the bully scene. What will he or she report to the teacher/the authorities?

And then one day one normal un-special day Adrienne comes to school and announces that it's penalty day. We don't know what penalty day is. Adrienne explains that on penalty day one girl is chosen and everyone is mean to that one girl for that one day.

— from *The Shape of a Girl* by Joan MacLeod

If any of you happens to see an injustice, you are no longer a spectator, you are a participant. And you have an obligation to do something.

— June Callwood

The trio can switch roles. The challenge is for the bystander to intervene. What might be said to the bully and/or the target to prevent this bullying incident from continuing?

READING SNIPPETS OUT LOUD

See page 60 for Bully Snippets.

The snippets featured on page 60 are suitable sources for both interpreting and improvising text. These lines of text have been excerpted from poems that are centred on the roles of the bully, the bullied, and the bystander.

The group sculpture is a useful strategy to use for ensemble presentations or assemblies. Students can make decisions about the most effective way to enter the scene. Adding music, props, or masks can enhance the theatrical presentation.

- Students randomly select one bully snippet from the page. Alternatively, students can sit in a circle and each snippet can be assigned. Once students have one focus snippet, they practice ways to read it aloud; e.g., whisper, shout, angry, frightened, as a question. Students establish eye contact with someone across the circle and say the line to that person. This can be repeated more than once.

Other sources can be used for this snippet activity to suit a theme explored in class:

- snippets from a script
- snippets from poems; students can highlight the snippets
- newspaper headlines
- voices in the head from an in-role character that has been explored
- graffiti

- In a circle, students read their lines of text out loud. How do they think the character might read the line? Continue until all snippets are read.
- Repeat the readings in one or more of the following ways. Students may need the security of reading the text from the page. However, through repeated activities, they should become familiar with the text.
  - Students stand as they say their lines.
  - Students add a gesture before or after saying their lines.
  - Students add a gesture and are invited to freeze their action.
  - Each student in turn shares his or her gesture only and freezes the position (no verbal text).
  - Students rearrange themselves in the circle. Students read their line, add a gesture, and freeze.
- Invite students to make a group sculpture using the snippets. Each student enters the space in the circle and says his or her line. They can add their gestures before or after saying the line. One the line is said, have each student create a still image. As each person enters the circle, he or she can choose a space to perform. Students can, if they wish, attach themselves in some way to someone who has previously entered the circle. The activity continues until each person has had a chance to recite a line. As a final activity, students repeat the final line and create a new final still image.
- Note: An alternative way for students to create the group sculpture is to enter and make the gesture only. Once all participants have entered the scene, each individual, in turn, can say his or her line and create a new gesture.

IMPROVISING FROM SNIPPETS

See page 60 for Bully Snippets.

- Have each student consider whether the snippet is told from the point of view of a bully, a bullied, or a bystander. Why might someone say this line? Students can share their responses in small groups.
- Randomly assign student partners. Have students create a still image with two characters. Once students are satisfied with their tableaux, the lines of text can be said out loud by each of the characters.

- Invite students to become the characters who might say these lines. To prepare for this, students imagine what happened to the person that would prompt them to have this thought. Partners can take turns to tell their stories in role. As the conversation continues, encourage students to ask questions to uncover the story and find out the person's feelings about what happened.
- Students work in groups of four; i.e., two sets of partners. One student from each pair can introduce his or her partner to the other pair by retelling the story that was just heard: i.e., Partner A tells Partner B's story; Partner B tells A's story.
- Groups of four can create a tableau that would show each of these characters. Challenge the students to come up with a *new* line of snippet text that would represent something that this character might say or how this character might feel.

Extensions

a) Students can use the snippets that have been assigned to them or another snippet featured on the page. Invite each student to add a thought to his or her snippet. This could be an idea before the snippet, after the snippet, or before and after the snippet.

b) Students can share their work with a partner. Invite students to create a free verse poem by rearranging their words randomly on the page. Remind students that, in free verse poetry, the number of words on a single line can vary. Also, students can play with the white spaces to complete a poem.

c) Students can read their new poems out loud as short monologues about a bully, bullied, or bystander.

d) Students can create a graffiti wall of bully snippets. The message that they put on this wall should be advice that they would give to someone who is a bully.

MOSQUITO

- Instruct the students, "If you were to write a poem about a bully, a target, or a bystander and there was an animal in this poem, what animal would you choose? Why?" Students can write their responses on a file card and then share with two or three others.
- In a circle, students become the animals they have considered for their bully poems. Students can become and show the animals one-by-one as the activity continues around the circle. Alternatively, this activity can have each student first become an animal that is a bully. The activity can be repeated by having each student become an animal that is a target/victim.
- As a group, discuss the choices that each student made. Encourage them to give reasons for the animals they chose.
- Students read the poem on page 61 independently.
- Invite the students to read "Mosquito" aloud chorally in one of the following ways:

  - Alternate reading. Teacher reads one line; group reads the second, and so on. Repeat, this time reversing parts.
  - Whole group reads the poem in unison.

Bully Snippets

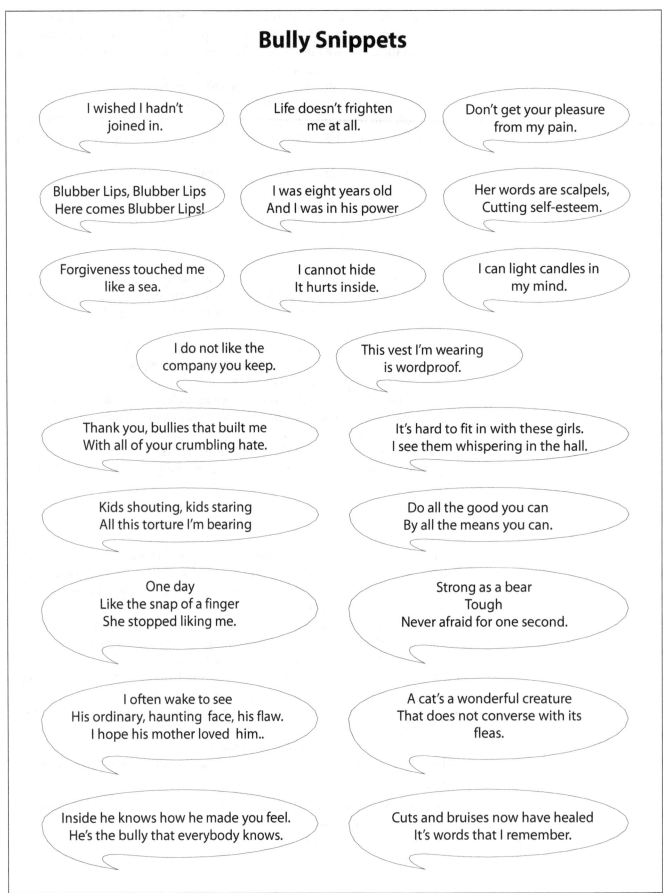

I wished I hadn't joined in.

Life doesn't frighten me at all.

Don't get your pleasure from my pain.

Blubber Lips, Blubber Lips Here comes Blubber Lips!

I was eight years old And I was in his power

Her words are scalpels, Cutting self-esteem.

Forgiveness touched me like a sea.

I cannot hide It hurts inside.

I can light candles in my mind.

I do not like the company you keep.

This vest I'm wearing is wordproof.

Thank you, bullies that built me With all of your crumbling hate.

It's hard to fit in with these girls. I see them whispering in the hall.

Kids shouting, kids staring All this torture I'm bearing

Do all the good you can By all the means you can.

One day Like the snap of a finger She stopped liking me.

Strong as a bear Tough Never afraid for one second.

I often wake to see His ordinary, haunting face, his flaw. I hope his mother loved him..

A cat's a wonderful creature That does not converse with its fleas.

Inside he knows how he made you feel. He's the bully that everybody knows.

Cuts and bruises now have healed It's words that I remember.

Pembroke Publishers ©2010 *Drama Schemes, Themes & Dreams* by Larry Swartz and Debbie Nyman ISBN 978-1-55138-253-1

Mosquito

by Larry Swartz

She's tiny.
She's mean.
She's cruel.
She fights.

The mosquito
   Buzzes.
The mosquito
   Bites.

She torments.
She swarms.
She teases.
She taunts.

The mosquito
   Buzzes
The mosquito
   Haunts.

You're bigger than her.
Your blood is what feeds.
Beware of the bully –
You're the victim she needs!

Pembroke Publishers ©2010 *Drama Schemes, Themes & Dreams* by Larry Swartz and Debbie Nyman ISBN 978-1-55138-253-1

- Poem is read as a round: group is divided in two; one group begins before the other.
- Each student, in turn, reads one of the lines.

- As a class, discuss why this poet chose to use a mosquito: How is a mosquito like a bully? What does this poem help us to think about bullies?

Extension

Some students may choose to write a bully poem using an animal as a metaphor. They can choose to have the poem rhyme or not.

CHORAL DRAMATIZATION

Unlike traditional scripts, where characters are assigned parts, choral dramatization has students determine which lines will be read as solo or in small groups.

Choral dramatization invites students to read aloud such texts as rhymes and poems by assigning parts among group members. By working with peers to read aloud poems on a particular theme or topic, or by a single poet, students take part in a creative activity that involves experimentation with voice, sound, gesture, and movement. Because of these variations, no two oral interpretations of a single poem are alike.

Choral dramatization enhances students' skills of read-aloud and presentation. More importantly, however, when students work in small groups to read a poem out loud, their problem-solving skills are likely to be enriched as they make decisions about the best way to present a poem.

It is most appropriate to have students prepare a presentation of the poems after they have explored ways to read poems aloud in a shared reading experience with the whole class. Students work in groups of three or four, and each group is given a poem to present chorally. Once the choral reading has been practiced, each group share its work. You could assign two groups the same text. When they present their work to each other, they can compare different interpretations.

Strategy Scheme: Ten Ways to Read a Poem Out Loud

1. INTRODUCE THE POEM

- Leader reads aloud without displaying the poem.
- Leader reads as participants follow along with their eyes.

2. ECHO READING

- Leader reads one line: the group echoes what the leader says.

3. ALTERNATE-LINE READING

- Leader reads one line, the group reads the second line; they continue alternating lines.
- The activity is repeated by reversing parts.
- This can also be done in pairs with partners reading alternate parts.

Under Attack

by Peter Jalaill

STOP! STOP!
I'm under attack
Don't call me that
I can't turn back.

STOP! STOP!
I'm under attack
Just landed here
So full of fear.

STOP! STOP!
I'm under attack
I have a name
I have a claim.

STOP! STOP!
I'm under attack
I cannot hide
It hurts inside

STOP! STOP!
I'm under attack
I have feelings too
Just like YOU!

4. CLOZE TECHNIQUE

- Leader reads each line, omitting the final world; the group joins in to say the word and complete the line.
- The activity can be repeated with the leader omitting additional words.

5. PITCH

- Read the poem in unison, starting in a whisper and gradually getting louder.
- Read the poem in unison, starting in a loud voice and gradually getting softer to a whisper.

6. PACE

- Read the poem in unison, starting slowly and gradually increasing speed.
- Read the poem in unison, starting quickly and gradually decreasing speed.

7. HAND CLAPPING

- The poem is read at a rhythmic pace, accompanied by clapping rhythm.
- Partners can play pat-a-cake while saying the poem together.

8. ROUND

- One group begins to say the poem in unison. The next group begins to say the poem in unison after the first group has finished the first line. Groups will finish at different times.
- The activity can be repeated with three or more groups.

9. ASSIGNING LINES

- Each person in the group is assigned a line, a part of a line, or a word.
- The group rehearses the poem, with each person contributing his or her part.

10. ONLY A WORD

- The group sits in a circle.
- The poem is read with each person reading one word in turn.

My Story/Your Story/Our Story: Building Inclusion through Drama Prompts
by Wendie Gibbons

As a beginning drama teacher, I understood the importance of building community and creating an insult-free environment in the drama classroom and carefully planned September with this focus in mind. My students participated in cooperative exercises, teambuilding activities, get-to-know you/learning name games, and lessons that helped develop listening and focusing skills. I was proud of taking the time to create a classroom environment where my students would feel safe and free to take risks.

Imagine my dismay when halfway through the year I discovered students had forgotten the names of their peers, that their cooperative, listening, and focusing skills had decreased, and that the "community" I had painstakingly creating had vanished. Clearly, they had forgotten what being a community meant, and it dawned on me how far away September was for these students. They needed an activity that was constant, that provided structure, that built on the foundation laid in September.

It was in my fourth year of teaching that I found my inspiration.

My students direct original plays for the Sears Ontario Drama Festival, and one day I walked into the beginning of a rehearsal to find the students sharing the highs and lows of their day. They asked me to join, which I did, and was surprised to see how honest and willing they were to share with each other. They did this activity at the start of every rehearsal. It was a simple bonding exercise that quickly established what kind of mood everyone was in and helped the company get to know each other quickly.

Recognizing the potential that these prompts had to massage each student's personal memory story bank, I decided to introduce conversation starters that I called "drama prompts," not only with the intention of uncovering personal narratives but also to build community as students chose to reveal their thoughts and feelings to others. At the start of the year, the prompts were simple: *I was looking forward/not looking forward to high school because…*; *I'm excited/ nervous about drama because…*; etc. Then, when the class grew more comfortable with each other, the prompts would challenge: *If I could change one thing about myself…*; *After an emotionally draining situation, I recharge myself by…*; etc. I would alternate the serious prompts with fun ones: e.g., *If you could have one superhero power, what would it be?*; *My favorite comfort food is….* At other times, the prompt would introduce a unit or drama structure: *Share a bullying story, either experienced or witnessed*; *A defining moment in my life was…*; etc.

The drama prompts proved a success. The students look forward to them, sometimes coming to class with prompts of their own. On field trip days or days when attendance dwindles, we do several prompts in a row, at their insistence. More than once, the prompts have become teachable moments and powerful experiences for both the students and myself.

Many drama teachers can choose to introduce their classes with a hot topic based on news from the media, school or community events, or opinions/reactions to a movie, play, or television program. I believe that the drama prompts provide a daily ritual that is both personal and communal. Every drama class now starts with the students sitting in a circle, awaiting the drama prompt to begin a conversation. The prompt is announced and I wait for hands to go up. I always call on people by name and thank them once they're finished, saying their name again. This way, names are reinforced over and over again, every single class. If someone else has created a prompt to share with the class, they run it, mimicking my manner. No one can answer until everyone is listening. Students have the right to pass, but I try to encourage them to answer as frequently as possible. After a while, it's easy to tell when a student isn't in the mood to answer or just can't think of anything to say.

I have learned a great deal about my students through these prompts: dreams, goals, death of a loved one, divorce, break-ups, sexual orientation, sickness, wants, likes and dislikes. I am more aware than ever what is important in their lives, what they watch on TV, what they are exposed to on YouTube, what music and lyrics they listen to, what they look for in a friend, what is fashionable, and what a good teacher looks like in their eyes. In return, they have learned about me: that I, too, am a student; that I lived in Korea; that I don't listen to music or watch TV but love movies and popcorn and green tea lattes. It is important that I am part of this story-sharing ritual, both as a model for telling stories and as a fellow community member. Two rules guide me:

1) I never ask a prompt I'm not prepared to answer myself, and
2) I always answer last. This is to avoid influencing anyone else's answer.

There are hidden benefits to students in the drama prompts, the ones only a drama teacher might realize: expressing oneself before an audience, articulating thoughts and feelings, telling stories, speaking loudly and clearly so everyone can hear, active listening, asking appropriate questions, and seeking clarification rather than jumping to conclusions. For the teacher, it's a significant way to discover what is interesting and relevant in the lives of students, what stresses they are experiencing, how capable they are of articulating their thoughts, and how successful they are at listening and responding to others.

Drama prompts have changed the dynamics of my classes. I do not have the discipline problems I used to have, students know each other's names, and they respect and appreciate each other's differences better. The experiences we have gone through have sometimes been life-changing. One student listened in awe as a student shared his story of leaving his war-torn country in the middle of the night; we heard a student share the news that her parents were breaking up; another told us her life-defining moment was when she realized her brother was gay. The environment we had created was clearly one where these students felt safe enough to share. I am very proud of how respectful, kind, and gracious my students have become, and am thrilled with the lasting community that has been created in my classes. I've heard Larry Swartz tell teachers that "the best response to a story is to tell another story." Not only is it exciting to have students tell stories that bounced off the stories of others, but I came to realize that such an event helps to organize —or reorganize —the students into a circle of caring citizens, a story tribe.

Extending the Drama Prompts

- After telling a personal story, students can record it in writing. These personal narratives can be shaped into monologue presentations.
- Students can share their story using tableau images, mime, or movement.
- Once a prompt has been offered, students can record their responses in writing. These stories can be shared and rehearsed with a partner, in small groups, or in the community circle.
- Encourage students to ask questions, once a story has been shared. From time to time, an opportunity can be given for group members to interview the teller.

A Drama Structure Using a Poem

Shame
by Tracey Blance

There's a girl at school
We teased her today;
Made jokes, called her names.
My friends all laughed,
called it harmless fun,
said it was just a game.

Now I'm at home
Feeling horrid inside,
Long gone that thoughtless grin.
How will I face her
Tomorrow at school?
I wish I hadn't joined in.

WHY DO YOU THINK YOU DID THAT?: QUESTIONING

After reading the poem independently, students were given file cards to list three questions that they would ask the girl who is "feeling horrid inside." Partners were formed and students compared questions. Each person was allowed to "borrow" one question from his or her partner.

Students worked in groups of four to compare questions to determine similarities and differences. The students were then challenged to prioritize the most important question they would ask this girl if she came into their classroom.

(with thanks to Vanessa Russell)

In the poem, we learn that the bullies "made jokes" and "called her [the bullied girl] names." The event described here challenged students to consider the issue of name-calling and put-downs. The instructions for this powerful event are as follows:

To prepare this activity, a large cutout shape of a human body is needed. One student can volunteer to lie down in a neutral position (arms and legs should be outstretched) on a large sheet of paper while a partner traces the outline of the body. This outline is then cut out.

Introduce the Crumple Person activity:

1. Have students sit in a circle. Introduce the cut-out human form to the group with a gender neutral name; e.g., Chris, Pat, Sandy.

2. Inform students that Chris is not doing well today at school. Chris has been harassed and bullied; over the week, Chris has been called a number of names that have been hurtful.

3. Students consider: What are some of the put-down names that Chris might have heard at school? Note: Some put-downs can be considered sensitive because of their sexual, racial, or cultural intent. This activity encourages students to be trusting of each other; they are invited to volunteer these names to help them consider the meaning and intent of the terms.

4. Invite students to volunteer to record a put-down term that Chris might have heard. Students are given a marker to write the term somewhere on the cutout body. With each derogatory name, the figure is crumpled once by the student who identified the put-down word.

5. The activity continues with volunteers coming forward. Some may choose to record more than one item. Some may choose to remain silent during the activity. Provide wait time for students to come forward.

6. As a final activity, Chris can be shown to each student. Students can choose to add a name or not.

7. Once the figure is entirely crumpled, ask students: How is Chris different from before? How do you think Chris feels? How do you think Chris might act or behave?

8. Ask students to consider how they might be able to help Chris feel better. What could the people at Chris's school say or do to help Chris? With each suggestion, invite a student to come forward and smooth over a place where Chris has been harmed. It is not necessary for students to uncrumple their own derogatory comment. The activity continues until Chris has been entirely uncrumpled.

9. Ask the students: How is Chris different from the beginning of the class? How might Chris feel now? Does Chris feel better? Discuss how Chris's "scars" or put-downs might have a visible and lasting effect.

10. Discuss with the class how we can ensure that no one gets "crumpled" in the class. What are some ground rules and group norms that need to be considered? Are these realistic? Can there be consequences if rules are broken?

11. Students record their feelings about the activity. How did this activity help them think about bullying behavior? How did this activity connect to their own experiences or to those of someone they know?

Extensions

a) Although the activity can be considered most powerful when shared with a group sitting in a circle, other teachers have done similar activities in the following ways:

- Students work alone or in small groups to write put-downs on a character figure.
- In lieu of crumpling, "tear" the cut-out figure. The scars can then be taped together.
- The activity can be done using nails hammered into a board. Each time a put-down is offered, students hammer a nail into a block of wood. The nails can be removed, with the holes left representing scars.

b) The Crumple Person activity can be the foundation of a writing-in-role activity. Students can write a letter from Chris's point of view, from someone who bullied Chris, or from a bystander who witnessed the put-downs. These letters can be exchanged and students can improvise a meeting between two characters at some future date in Chris's life.

I WISH I HADN'T JOINED IN: IMPROVISATION

To explore backward and forward in time from the bullying incident described in the poem, students worked in small groups, each given a scenario to improvise.

Scenario #1: *Earlier that day*
Dramatize what you think happened to the girl at school. To prepare for this improvisation, consider what prompted the bullying incident. Did everyone in the group join in the teasing?

Scenario #2: *That night*
The girl, sitting in her room, decides that she needs to talk to someone (a parent, sibling, friend, neighbor, etc.) about what happened. How much will she confess? What advice might someone give the girl?

Scenario #3: *The next day*
What happens when the girls meet up the next day at school? To prepare for this improvisation, consider things that the bully might say to make the target feel better. Will an apology work? How might the girl react?

Scenario #4: *A few weeks later*
Another bullying incident occurs. This time the first-person girl in the poem decides not to join in. As a bystander, what things might she say or do to prevent the bullying incident from continuing? How might she convince others to stop their actions?

Scenario #5: *Twenty years later*

Twenty years have passed. The girls in the poem meet at a school reunion. What conversation might take place between the girl who was bullied and the girl who felt horrid inside?

CULMINATING ACTIVITY: A BULLIED GIRL'S BLOG

Students were provided with a copy of blog messages sent to Christina (see page 69). After reading the messages silently, students shared their reactions to these messages with a friend: What do we learn about each of the authors who wrote? What advice might you give Christina?

Students worked independently to write a blog message in role. For this activity, students considered writing a message that might be sent by Christina. Alternatively, students could send another blog message that each of these characters might write.

Once the blog-in-role was completed, students worked in pairs to exchange written messages. Students each read messages in role as Christina. Students were invited to select one line of text that they think best had an impact on the bullied girl.

Students gathered in an inner- and outer-circle formation. Those on the outside circle worked in role as Christina, and each in turn read one line of text from her blog. Those on the inside of the circle spoke in role as someone who wrote the message, considering these ideas: Why did they send this message? What did they hope would be gained by sending a blog message? What action could be taken by Christina?

A final class discussion about The Bully, The Bullied, and the Bystander took place. The following three questions framed the discussion:

- Why does a bully behave the way he or she does?
- How can we give the bullied courage to stand up to the bully?
- What role does the bystander play in the bullying triangle?

Extending the Drama

WRITING IN ROLE

Students can use one of the following contexts for writing in role as an extension of the drama work:

- Bully, who feels horrid, writes a letter of apology to the person he/she teased.
- Bully writes a diary entry that night that describes his/her feelings about joining in the teasing incident.
- Students write a poem from the point of view of the girl who was being teased at school. How can they twist the ideas in Tracey Blance's poem to show the target's point of view?
- Students write in role as a parent of bullied student. As mothers or fathers, they write a letter to school authorities, a bully's parent, or their daughter.
- Write messages for a Facebook wall for a person who has been bullied.

Blog Messages

Blog 1: Should have/Could have/Would have

You don't know me and I would sort of like to keep it that way. I saw you and I have been there when they called you names. I know they picked on you but it wasn't my fault. I didn't do anything. I should have tried to stop them. I could have tried to stop them. I would have tried to stop them but… should've, could've, would've

Blog 2: Trying to Catch Up

I wish that I could have gone to you, helped you up when they you pushed you down. I even wish that I had just stayed behind to talk to you. I just kept moving. I felt all hot and weak, and so afraid, so I just kept walking, hoping like always that no one would notice me or see me. Perhaps next time I'll be braver. Be strong.

   PS: I am in your gym class. I am the one running behind always trying to catch up.

Blog 3: Next Time?

I should have done something
You don't know me but I have seen you, seen them, you know. I heard those names. I just kept walking. Because you know it could have been me. It has been me. I wanted to help you up. I really did, but my heart was racing, I couldn't breathe. I wish… Maybe next time?

   By: You don't know me (I promise)

Blog 4: My Daughter is Being Bullied

I know she is being bullied. I can just tell. She is sad, stays in her room for hours alone, won't talk about it. I know the stories followed her to high school. She thought it would be over after middle school. The same kids, always the same kids. And it doesn't end at school. Text messages, Facebook. There is nowhere for her to go to escape. I am so sorry she is hurting so bad. I wonder if I let this happen. I lie in bed and wonder what to do, what to do.

Blog 5: Wanna trade places?

What would you have done if you were in my shoes? Who doesn't want to be part of the in-crowd in order to be protected? Don't you think you could just play the game?

Blog 6: Advice

Consider this a warning. I know that what is written in a blog does not stay in a blog.

   You asking for advice? My advice is to put an end to this blog right now. Don't be asking for pity or attention. Don't get in our way again. My advice? Stop asking for advice.

Pembroke Publishers ©2010 *Drama Schemes, Themes & Dreams* by Larry Swartz and Debbie Nyman ISBN 978-1-55138-253-1

Script Variation: Public Service Announcement

CREATE A PUBLIC SERVICE ANNOUNCEMENT

A Public Service Announcement (PSA) is an advertisement broadcast on radio, TV, or the Internet for the public interest that is intended to change public attitudes by raising awareness and educating the public about specific issues.

1. Invite the students to work in groups and create a list of understandings that they have learned about bullying from the drama work. They should focus on the understandings they feel other students and/or teachers and parents should have about the issue. Students share their lists and create one list together that represents their concerns about the issue.
2. You can gather facts and information about bullying from a number of websites and print resources (see reference list on page 170) to offer students. This factual information can be used as support for students to create an announcement. Some facts include:

   - Bullying occurs in school playgrounds every seven minutes and once every 25 minutes in class. (Wendy Craig and Debora Pepler)
   - There is a small but significant co-relation between parental aggression and bullying. Glenn Di Pasquale)

Concerned Children's Advertisers is committed to creating and delivering marketing campaigns to assist children understand the challenges they face, including social issues and media literacy issues. The website includes pertinent information for children, parents, and teachers.

Invite the students to view Public Service Announcements on YouTube, specifically from Concerned Children's Advertisers: e.g., Words Hurt, The Bully, Tell Someone

3. After viewing the public service announcement, invite students to analyze and reflect using the following questions:

   - Which of the understandings that you listed were brought to life in this video?
   - Who is represented in the piece? Is everyone represented fairly and realistically?
   - With whom do you sympathize and why?
   - What points of view are missing? Do you think they should have been included?
   - How did the creators use the following to make their statement?
     Sound
     Words and dialogue
     Camera angles
     Music
   - What changes would you want to make to this piece?
   - Why is the Public Service Announcement an effective format for informing the public about bullying?

   Students can work in groups and select an understanding from the list that they feel could be effectively shared through a PSA.

4. To prepare a PSA, students need to develop a script that would include narration, dialogue, description of scenes, camera shots, etc. Some students might prepare a storyboard to help them plan their PSA. The challenge is to have the PSA be no longer than 60 seconds. To be considered:

- What fact(s) have they encountered that support what they wish to communicate?
- Who is the audience for this announcement: i.e., parents, peers, administrators?
- What would be the best setting for this announcement?
- What would be the most intriguing image to begin the announcement? To conclude?
- How might music/sound enhance the mood and intention of the piece?
- How will they vary the camera angles to convey their message effectively?.

5. Once prepared, students can prepare a pitch for this PSA by sharing it with another group. They should be prepared to describe their announcement and persuade others of the significance of this work.

At this stage students should experiment with ways to create a final product. This involves rehearsing, revising, directing, and performing to an audience. Because of the brevity of the product, students should be encouraged to create a number of versions of their announcements.

Students might bring in cameras, use a school camera, or use the technology on their phones.

6. Final products can be shared with an audience. An opportunity for responding critically to the work (see questions above) should be introduced.

Assessment: Choral Dramatization Checklist

Name _____ Date _____

Does the student…	Consistently	Sometimes	Not Yet
• use voice appropriately to convey mood and intent?	☐	☐	☐
• recognize his or her role in the ensemble?	☐	☐	☐
• contribute ideas to the choral presentation?	☐	☐	☐
• support the contributions of others?	☐	☐	☐
• have an appropriate sense of audience?	☐	☐	☐
• follow directions and accept advice?	☐	☐	☐
• experiment with pitch, pause, and pace to make the reading more effective?	☐	☐	☐
• investigate a variety of possibilities for using voice, sound, and movement?	☐	☐	☐
• understand the significance of revising/rehearsing?	☐	☐	☐
• seem committed to the task?	☐	☐	☐

Comments

Pembroke Publishers ©2010 *Drama Schemes, Themes & Dreams* by Larry Swartz and Debbie Nyman ISBN 978-1-55138-253-1

Who Put the Words in my Mouth?

Whether it be their less-threatening nature, their entertainment component, or their high-interest topics, comics are engaging. Because they are engaging, they often can perk up our passive readers and offer them the experience of what it feels like to be an active participant in the reading process — a feeling that, regrettably, many of them have never had before.
—Terry Thompson, *Adventures in Graphica*

Drama Theme: Communication

Using comics and graphic texts in the educational framework of literacy development offers opportunities to address issues of comprehension, fluency, content-area learning, vocabulary development, and wide reading. The graphic-novel format offers an excellent source for dramatic interpretation, as students read the words of the narration or speech bubbles. The visual images also provide material for creating still images or action sequences drawn from the panels created by the artist. Readers also need to read between the lines, between the panels, to bring meaning to the narrative; in this way, they can improvise dramatic situations that may not be depicted on the printed page.

Graphic novels offer high-interest reading to many at-risk and reluctant readers who usually shun traditional texts, as well as to proficient readers who search for an engaging genre. Graphic texts are particularly helpful for English Language Learners. The visual messages placed alongside the minimal printed text remove some of the blocks that may frustrate struggling readers who are attempting to comprehend the text and process the story. The effectiveness of graphic texts for creating proficient readers is directly related to the way that they are constructed. The pictures not only support the text but are also part of the text. The written words themselves are artistically placed and drawn to enhance the reader's capability to make meaning. Readers are given context clues within the subtle (and sometimes not so subtle) expressions, symbols, and actions of the characters.

LEARNING OPPORTUNITIES

- To develop and practice comprehension strategies with at-risk, reluctant, and proficient readers
- To recognize students' reading choices outside school and complete them with the texts introduced in school
- To use graphic texts as sources for writing scripts

- To role-play characters and improvise situations that are featured in graphic texts
- To develop interpretation skills by reading the verbal text (narration and conversation) that appears in graphic texts
- To develop rehearsal and presentation as students interpret and improvise graphic texts

Launching the Drama: Communication Games

1. I AM A TREE

- Students are organized in groups of four or five. One pre-group is chosen to create a still image of a tree. One student recites the line "I am a tree!"
- One of the members of the group enters the scene, adding on to the tree image in some way (e.g., a leaf) and recites the line, "I am a leaf."
- A third person adds on to the scene (e.g., a caterpillar) and recites the line, "I am a caterpillar."
- The tree then decides whether he or she will keep the leaf or the caterpillar. If neither is chosen, the two items go back to the group and the activity is repeated.
- Any group member can decide how to add on to the scene. The person who began the image is always the one who makes the decision about which item(s) they will keep, once a three-figure tableau has been created. Encourage students to be as spontaneous as possible to develop the tableau. The game continues for 5 to 10 minutes. Students can share some of the unique items they've pretended to be.

Extensions

a) The game is played sequentially in a circle. Player #1 makes an image, quickly followed by player #2 and player #3. Player number #4 creates a completely new image, followed by #5 and #6. Each player should recite the line "I am a _____."
b) The game is played with the whole class standing in the circle. One player volunteers to go in the middle to create an image. Anyone from the circle can decide to enter the scene. The game continues until a tableau of five people is created.

2. COMIC CONVENTION

- Invite students to think of a character from daily comic strips or comic books that they like or admire. Tell students to imagine that a convention of comic characters will be held and that each person is allowed to bring one guest — i.e., character from a comic — to the convention.
- On a signal, students wander around the room and introduce their guests to anyone they meet.
- At each introduction, students exchange guests, keeping the new character they will host until encountering another person. It is acceptable for each person to meet a character more than once, since he or she will have a chance to pass on the guest again.

Katie to Alex: "I'd like you to meet Jughead."
Alex to Katie: "I have the Joker standing beside me and I'd like you to meet him."
Katie takes the Joker and Alex takes Jughead. Alex next meets Laura.
Alex to Laura: "Laura, I'd like you to meet Jughead."
Laura to Alex: "And this is Professor Xavier."
Alex takes Professor Xavier, and Laura takes Jughead. They move on to the next encounter.

- After a few minutes, stop the activity and have each person tell who he or she brought to the party. Ask students to find out who presently has that guest.
- The game might cause some confusion for some students the first time it is played, so it could be repeated in one or more of these ways:
  - At a convention of novel characters
  - At a convention of historical characters
  - At a convention of heroes

Extensions

a) Provide each student with a file card or piece of paper. Invite students to write short diary entries from the point of view of the character they brought to the convention.
b) Once students have written their fictional diary entries, they can exchange them with a friend. Partners conduct an interview to find out more information about the comic character and deepen the role that has been assumed.
c) The class decides which two characters brought to the convention should meet. Discuss with the class which two characters would be interesting to put together, where they might meet, when they might meet, and how the meeting will develop. Two people can volunteer to role-play the characters, and the improvisation can develop using a forum theatre technique, where the group offers suggestions about how conversations might continue.

3. KNOCK! KNOCK!

Jokes and riddles are ideal for a comic-strip format featuring speech bubbles.

Since a *Knock! Knock!* joke involves two characters, each taking a turn with a line of dialogue, they are ideal for creating an instant graphic page. By folding a piece of paper twice (once horizontally, and once vertically), students create four panels to illustrate their joke. The punch line can be put on the back of the page.

Knock! Knock! jokes also are suitable sources for interpreting, rehearsing, and presenting a minimal script. Students can work in pairs to rehearse and present a *Knock! Knock!* of their choice. Encourage partners to take turns rehearsing each of the parts. As students practice the presentation, they can make consider

- How will each person, stand, sit, move?
- How will each person read the dialogue? (i.e., pace, pause and pitch)
- How will they end the joke? (i.e. a final image to complete the joke or the punch line).

Extension

Once each pair has rehearsed the presentation of their joke, an order can be decided for presenting the jokes to create and perform an instant collective.

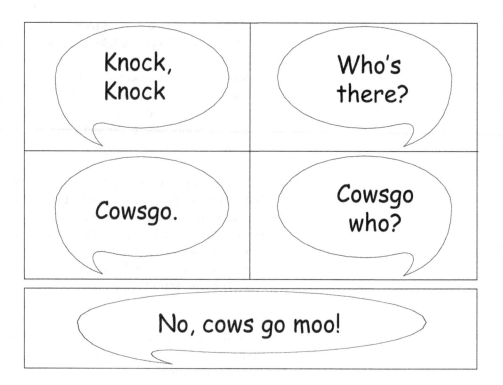

4. DRAMATIZING COMIC STRIPS

The dialogue and concise situations that are provided in comic strips are ideal for instant dramatization.

This activity might work best with strips featuring two characters.

- Students work in pairs to dramatize three or four panels of a comic strip. Each partner decides the role he or she is playing.
- Students read the script aloud, each having a chance to read either character.
- Students add action to the script. How will the characters, stand, sit or move? Some students may wish to use props for their dramatization.

Extensions

a) Pairs can add dialogue to what might appear before (or after) the conversation that is shown in the comic strip. Students can prepare a short improvisation that includes the original scripted dialogue.

b) The can be repeated using a longer comic strip that appears on a half or full page of a newspaper. Two or more characters can appear in these scenarios.

YouTube: A New Source for Drama
by Jill Lloyd-Jones, freelance drama and dance educator

As with many teachers of my generation, born before the computer was invented, it has been an ongoing (but enjoyable!) challenge for me to keep my teaching meaningful and accessible in an ever-changing landscape of technological advancements. My knowledge and teaching practice originated in books and, in my world, it was birds that "tweeted" and "twittered," not students. In the past year, I was invited into many classes to teach young adolescents. A heart-stopping realization overcame me—I was out of touch, what once worked brilliantly now felt flat and outdated. There was a generation gap—or should I say, chasm—and it was visibly widening, as was the variety of cultures and experiences of my students.

For most students, it is the Internet, not books, that has become the hub of what is original and thought-provoking, where questions are asked and answered, and where the resulting information becomes real. With students' ever-changing knowledge of technology, and as texting has replaced passing notes in class, comes my responsibility to provide a classroom curriculum that is current and relevant, one in which students can see themselves and their lives reflected. This propelled my exploration of YouTube to find some new non-print sources to explore in drama.

To begin, I signed up to see if there was anything that might fit in with my curriculum plans for the year. I was overwhelmed by the sheer mass of content but, after experimenting with phrases, I stumbled on using keywords: *environment, global warming*, etc. A fabulous array of sources emerged. Then I discovered an interesting Greenpeace advertorial: "Angry Kid," a monologue of a disaffected and angry young man blaming adults for not doing enough about global warming, and threatening to do something about it, or else! I e-mailed Greenpeace, requesting permission to use it for educational use, and downloaded it to my computer.

To build belief prior to presenting the source, I asked students to use Defining the Space (see page 41) to create a school staffroom. Then, with the students in role as teachers, I entered in role as the principal and presented the problem for discussion of a missing student, expressing major concerns about his safety. Out of role, I distributed an image of the young man and invited students to determine what they felt they knew, what they wanted to know, and what they could interpret and/or predict from the image. We documented responses as a collective using Role on the Wall (see page 82).

Continuing in role, I presented a garbage bag full of artifacts from the young man's locker to provide clues as to what might be happening in his life. To prepare for this I had created the artifacts ahead of time: a diary with a few cryptic entries; a child's birthday card from an absent Dad; a baseball with a loving message "*from Mum*" written on it; a couple of crumpled ecology posters; and a handwritten map. In role, students tried to make sense of the items and what they might mean. To move the drama along, I added that we all had had experiences with this student, and perhaps would know of an important event that would have shaped who he is. Then I created heterogeneous groups and invited them to share their imagined event in a frozen image (tableau). Back in role as principal, I stated that the school had just received a disturbing communication—a final video from the boy that I was going to share on my computer. As students clustered around, there was a palpable atmosphere of excitement!

I then used Corridor of Voices (see page 26). I instructed: "It sounds as if he is going to take the law into his own hands. What advice would you give him on what to do next?" A student volunteered to walk slowly down the corridor in role as the young man, to listen to the advice, and to choose to respond or not. At the end of the corridor, with everyone in total silence, he turned and said, "Why should I believe you now?"

That powerful moment emerged because of our separate understanding of the YouTube visual (their world) juxtaposed with the text of the source (my world). As our two worlds entwined, my respect for the power of technology as source material for my students has created a compelling paradigm for my future drama teaching.

Framing the Theme: Interpreting Words and Pictures

JUDGE A BOOK BY ITS COVER

Often, we choose the books we read for the cover, which is often dependent on the appeal of verbal text and art. The color and size of the image, the symbolic or narrative power depicted on the front of the book, can invite (or dismiss) readers as they make connections to the title or picture, make predictions, and raise questions about what is going to happen in the book.

A graphic novel, in particular, relies on a balance of verbal and visual cues. Encourage readers to spend time examining the cover to help analyze information and make predictions about what the book is about. The following prompts may be useful for students to respond to individually, with a partner, or in small groups.

- I see…
- I hear…
- I like…

- I think the character(s) might be saying/thinking…
- This image reminds me of…
- I think the storyline might be…
- I am curious about…
- I want to find out…
- The important characters in this story are…
- The main setting of this story is…

Five ways to build drama using a cover page:

1. Tableaux: Physically recreating the image on the front cover: *What are three images that you think might appear in the story? Consider Beginning, Middle, End.*
2. Thought Tracking: Adding a voice: *What might the character be saying/thinking?*
3. Interviewing: Brainstorming questions that might be asked of the character: Conduct an interview in pairs, in small groups, or with the whole class.
4. Storytelling: Using cues from the front cover, students work collaboratively to invent a story. Share the story in or out of role or as story theatre.
5. Illustrating: Create a comic-strip frame that would show one scene in the story: *What might the characters do? What might they say?* Once the illustration is completed, dramatize the scene using dialogue.

NARRATIVE CAPTIONS

Captions are featured in a graphic story to help the reader understand what is happening. A caption often helps to fill a gap in the story and can explain what is drawn in the frame or frames that appear on that page. Captions are useful in helping readers understand the passing of time as the story unfolds.

- Using the sample narrative captions from a graphic story, students visualize and, in pairs, make predictions about what pictures they expect to go with each caption. Partners work to create a still image to accompany each caption.

Sample One: adapted from *Amazing Greek Myths of Wonders and Blunders* by Michael Townsend
- Greek Mythology is full of strange and funny-looking creatures.
- There are valiant heroes…
- Nasty monsters…
- And people in need of heroes because of nasty monsters.
- Not to forget the kings and their soldiers who worked hard to protect their kingdoms.
- Last but not least, the immortal gods
- Who lived together in a beautiful palace on top of Mount Olympus.

Sample Two: from *Shadow World* by Robert Cutting
- John Tanaka visits his best friend Billy Fordham, after receiving an urgent phone message.
- Billy slowly opens his bedroom door.
- The door disappears.

- Students can create an improvised scene to show what they think is happening in the story: What will the setting be? Who are the characters? What will they say? What will they be doing?
- Students can create an illustration to accompany one of the captions.

By incorporating the graphic novel into school literacy programs, educators will be recognizing students' reading choices outside school and completing them with the texts mandated inside school.

—David Booth and Kathy Lundy, *In Graphic Detail*

Often the writer and illustrator for a graphic text are two different people. A graphic story can be considered successful if both the words and the story bring a balance of meaning to the text.

The author's words are often submitted in script format. He or she can make suggestions about the layout of the page (i.e., the number of panes, the arrangement of frames, etc.) but it is the artist who imagines and interprets the visual images that will appear on the page.

Students imagine that they have been hired as an illustrator of a graphic story. They can use the sample script as information to create a comic page for a script. Students should consider the use of close-ups and panoramic views for their illustrations. How many characters will appear in each frame?

Excerpt from *Danny King of the Basement* by David Craig:

PENELOPE: Hey, are you okay?

ANGELO: Your feet must be so cold.

DANNY: They're okay.

PENELOPE: Why do you wear those boots? They're so old-fashioned.

DANNY: They're okay.

PENELOPE: I wouldn't wear them if you paid me.

DANNY: They're okay, okay?

ANGELO: Yeah, who cares!

PENELOPE: I think I've been nice long enough. (She turns and leaves)

Extension

Novels are useful sources for creating graphic texts. Students can choose a page from a novel to transform into one or two graphic pages. A class project might have students working independently to create a graphic text, but pictures can be organized to create a graphic-novel version of a favorite novel. Encourage students to use features of a graphic page, including close-ups, medium shots, landscape views, speech bubbles, thought bubbles, narrative captions, sound effects, etc.

Some wordless picture books:

Anno's Journey by Mitsumasa Anno

Home by Jeannie Baker

Zoom by Istvan Banyai

Picturescape by Elisa Gutierrez

No! by David McPhail

Why? by Nikolai Popos

The Invention of Hugo Cabret by Brian Selznick

The Arrival by Shaun Tan

Imagine a Night (trilogy) by Sarah L. Thomson; paintings by Rob Gonsalves

GIVING VOICE TO WORDLESS TEXTS

Often the pages in a graphic text feature wordless texts. Readers need to make meaning from the visuals, using a number of strategies. A wordless text is very rich for drama exploration, since students can make personal interpretations of the narrative that is conveyed. Working collaboratively, students can share their personal hypotheses, hitch-hike off each other's interpretations, and share ideas to build a community story.

Provide students with a series of four to six illustrations that appear in a picture book. Challenge the students, working in groups, to arrange the pictures in a sequential order that they think tells a story. A more sophisticated approach is to have students decide the distance between each of the images to convey the amount of time passed, or to use overlapping images to suggest simultaneous events.

Strategy Scheme: Ten Ways to Work with Graphic Texts Dramatically

1. READERS THEATRE

Readers theatre is a dramatic reading for which students are assigned to read both the narration and dialogue of a story. Since the focus of readers theatre is the words, the use of gestures and props is kept to a minimum. Once students have identified their parts (one or more can be assigned to read narration), they need to practice different ways that a character might say the words. Students can rehearse and present a favorite graphic story as readers theatre. Note: longer graphic stories can be divided amongst different groups.

2. ACT IT OUT

Graphic stories are ideal for dramatization, since students can become the characters on the page, and say the words written in the speech bubbles. Challenge the students to represent the different scenes in a graphic story as closely as possible to the words and images featured in each panel. Groups can present the story in sequential order, frame by frame. A signal, such as a clap or a drumbeat, can be used to make changes from scene to scene.

3. IN-BETWEEN TIME

A graphic artist makes choices about which scenes will be included to tell the story. Often there is a gap in time between one frame and the next. As readers, we can infer what is happening in the story.

Invite students to examine a graphic text closely and discuss scenes that they think might be happening between two different panels. Students can work in small groups to improvise scenes that might have been included in the graphic story.

4. INTERVIEWING CHARACTERS

Students imagine that they have a chance to interview a character from a graphic story. They work in pairs or small groups to conduct an interview to find out about the characters' experiences. To prepare for this activity, have students brainstorm reasons why this character might be in an interview situation; i.e., what role will the interviewer take? The activity can be repeated with students switching roles and/or interviewing other characters.

5. TABLEAU PLAYS

Students physically recreate visual images from a graphic story to make tableaux. Encourage students to pay close attention to the position, gesture, and facial expression of each of the characters in the scene. Consideration should also be given to the blocking of one or more characters. Groups can create short tableau plays of a graphic story using four or five still images. Tableaux can be arranged sequentially to show the beginning, middle, and end of the story. A narrative caption can be read aloud to designate each tableau scene.

6. FACE TO FACE

A graphic artist is able to convey a lot of information in the facial expression of the characters in a story. Invite the students to examine the expressions on the characters' faces and discuss: What is each character feeling? How are the eyes different in each scene? How is the mouth different in each scene?

Working in pairs, students re-create these facial expressions to convey the feelings of the character. Each student can "direct" his or her partner to re-create the character as he/or she appears in a number of scenes.

7. INNER VOICES

The speech bubbles that appear in graphic texts provide readers with a character's dialogue. We might not, however, not get to know what a character is thinking.

Students add a *thought* to each of the character's dialogue speech bubbles, thus showing the inner voice of the character. Students can re-create the dialogue from one or more graphic novel scenes. As each person says his or her line, someone can suggest what the thoughts (i.e. inner voice) of the character might be

8. IMPROVISATION

Once students are familiar with the plot of a graphic story, groups can improvise scenes that would tell the story, or part of the story. Encourage students to use their own dialogue and improvise the action that would be used to tell the story.

9. DANCE DRAMA

Although a graphic story is told with verbal text and visual images, challenge the students to tell part of a graphic story nonverbally. To begin, students create tableau images that would be used to retell the story. Students then transition from scene to scene by moving in slow motion. By adding musical accompaniment to the movement pieces, students can create a dance drama based on a graphic text.

10. STORYTELLING

Students sit in a group to retell a graphic story. Students can each offer one or two sentences to tell the story sequentially. Encourage students to include as many details as possible to describe what happens and what is said in the story. Once the telling is completed, students can revisit the story to determine details that have been omitted or changed. The activity can be repeated by having the students tell the story in role from the point of view of one of the characters.

A Drama Structure Using a Graphic Novel

The following structure provides a framework for working with a graphic novel of your choice. The lesson described here uses the autobiographical novel *Persepolis* by Marjane Satrapi. A graphic text, like any resource, can offer a springboard for improvising and role-playing from the text. This outline is a useful way to start, with an image to build a context, a selected excerpt to interpret the text, and an improvised lesson that invites students to work in role to explore the theme of the book.

WHAT'S THE STORY?: PREVIEWING THE TEXT

Students were shown the cover of the book. The students responded to words and visual image by discussing the following: *What is your first impression of the name Persepolis? Who or what is Persepolis? What questions come to mind when you consider the title and the picture? What are your predictions about this story? How does the border used on the title page give you a cue to the story? What words would you use to describe the girl on the cover?*

WHO ARE YOU?: ROLE ON THE WALL

In Role on the Wall, the outline of the girl was placed on a large sheet of paper. Students were given sticky notes in two colors. On one color, students placed words that they felt would describe this girl. On a second color, each student listed a question he or she might ask this girl. These were arranged on the outside of the figure. This was done as a whole-class activity, where each person in turn approached the figure. (Note: the Role on the Wall activity can be adapted to be done independently or in small groups.)

PICTURE THIS: INTERPRETING A SINGLE VISUAL IMAGE

Students were offered a single visual image without words (displayed on a large screen).

Students were each given a file card and completed the following sentence stems:

- I see...
- I remember...
- I wonder...

Students, in pairs, exchanged cards and discussed their responses. Partners then matched up in groups of four. Attention was focused on the statement "I wonder..." to determine similar or different curiosities that came to mind. Students were given time to brainstorm other ideas that they wondered about.

A tableau image was spontaneously made to re-create the two-dimensional image. Students were invited to approach the tableau one-by-one. Each student revealed an "I wonder..." statement out loud. If there were two or three characters, students stood behind the character they wondered about.

DO YOU SEE WHAT I SEE?: WORKING WITH MULTIPLE VISUAL IMAGES

Single images from the graphic text were selected. These were displayed in the centre of a large chart. Charts were arranged in various areas of the room.

Students did a walkabout, in silence, to examine each of the illustrations. Students were then invited to remain at a single chart that intrigued them. Students were given an opportunity to work independently to add words, sentences, or images to the chart. These could reveal the feelings, questions, or connections that came to mind as they examined the image from the graphic novel.

Students were asked to respond to the responses of others. Time was given for students to wander around the room and examine charts other than the one they originally worked on. Students could add words or images in response to what others wrote or drew.

Students returned to their original source. As a group, students discussed what patterns or connections they could interpret from what was now on the chart.

GRAPHIC PAGE OUT LOUD: READERS THEATRE

Students worked with pages 78 and 79 from the graphic novel *Persepolis* by Marjane Satrapi.

Students worked with an excerpt from the graphic novel. They were invited to use this script to rehearse and present a readers theatre presentation. To begin, students decided the number of characters that appeared in the excerpt, and considered the number of narrators needed. Students collaborated to select parts that they would read out loud. After an initial rehearsal, students were invited to switch roles so that they had an opportunity to read a different part.

Once comfortable with their roles, students developed a readers theatre presentation to share with others. With readers theatre, students relied on a handheld script (displayed in a folder). Students were reminded that the way they interpreted the lines of text were particularly significant, since movement and gesture were kept to a minimum. Students shared their work with others by presenting the scenes in chronological order as they appear in the novel.

Reflection

- Were the students familiar with their parts?
- How successful were the students at reading narration or reading dialogue out loud fluently?
- Did the students work diligently to rehearse their presentation by experimenting with ways to read the text out loud? By making suggestions to others in the group?
- What theatre elements (e.g., voice, gesture, props, staging) were included to make the presentation interesting?

- How successful were the students at presenting readers theatre to an audience (i.e., awareness of audience, eye contact, projection and clarity)?

ANY QUESTIONS?: INQUIRY

To find out more about the character of Marjane, students were given an opportunity to hot-seat a character from the novel. To prepare for this activity, small groups brainstormed a list of questions that they might ask one of the characters in the story. Groups were each assigned a character to focus on; e.g., Marjane, her parents, a best friend or neighbor. Time was given for the students to list 15–20 questions. The students were then invited to highlight the three most significant questions. A representative from each group shared the questions from their chart, and these were recorded.

THE LIFE OF AN IRAQI TEENAGER: COLLECTIVE CHARACTER

Students had the opportunity to interview the characters. For this activity, the students worked collectively in role. The teacher, in role as media reporter, approached the group. Individuals in the group could volunteer to answer the reporter's questions by explaining what they knew, sharing an anecdote, or giving an opinion. It was important that that the group listen carefully to the answers given and build a focused understanding from the character's point of view.

MARJANE'S STORY: REVISITING ROLE ON THE WALL

Students revisited the role-on-the-wall image to consider new words and new questions that they had about this character.

FLASHBACK/FLASHFORWARD

This activity had students consider the actions they have chosen. A flashback invites students to imagine what might have preceded the present situation. A flashforward is an activity that encourages participants to think about the consequences of the relationships or actions they have chosen.

Students worked in groups of four and chose to improvise a flashback or flashforward scene to explain an event in Marjane's life. Students could choose to explore the distance in the past or the future. The intention of the scene was to demonstrate a decision or pivotal moment that led to the present (flashback) or a scene that to show one possible outcome of the action (flashforward).

Once prepared, students shared their work to help us understand the life of Marjane. Note: The teacher determined the order of the scenes chronologically by checking in with the students about the choices they made.

CULMINATING ACTIVITY

Using information that was presented in the improvisation, students created a new page of graphic text that could have appeared in the graphic novel. Students had the choice of working independently or with a partner to create a comic-strip page. They were encouraged to use the features of a graphic text, considering narrative captions, dialogue balloons, thought balloons, close-up scenes, panoramic views, etc.

Extending the Drama

The following activities can be used with a range of graphic texts.

CONTINUING THE STORY

Students make predictions about what might happen after the story is completed. Students can create one or more graphic pages to continue the story. These pages can be used as sources for enacting the story.

WRITING NARRATIVE

Students can retell the graphic story that they've read as a narrative piece of writing.

WRITING IN ROLE

Have students pretend that they are one of the characters in the graphic story. What might this character write in a diary or journal? Who might the character write a letter to? Why?

SUMMARIZING

Challenge students to write a summary of a graphic story they have read. Students can be further challenged to write the summary in 100 words or less, or 50 words or less. Or give students an exact number of words (e.g. 35). As an alternative, students can summarize the story visually using three to five panels.

SUMMARIZING THE CHAPTERS

Several graphic stories for young readers are divided into chapters. Students summarize what happens by writing three to five sentences for each chapter.

ADDING ILLUSTRATIONS

Students add frames that might have been included in the graphic story. In particular, they can create an illustration that might appear between two frames. What might the in-between picture be?

ELIMINATING ILLUSTRATIONS

Students work with one or two others to discuss which illustrations might be eliminated from the story if space was limited. Does the verbal text give enough information?

STORYBOARD

A storyboard is a convenient way to summarize the events of a story. Students can retell the story using three to five storyboard illustrations that highlight key events in the story. Storyboards are used by a director of a movie to prepare for the filming of the story. Students imagine that the graphic story they have read is going to be made into a film. They create a series of storyboard images that would help a director with his or her filmmaking. Encourage the students to use the following in their storyboards: close-ups, medium shots, panoramic views.

INVENTING A SEQUEL

Students use the characters from a graphic story to create a new story with those characters. What new problem or adventure might the characters have? Once students decide upon a story, they can create an improvisation that would feature the characters in a new story.

SOUNDTRACK

A common feature of graphic stories is the inclusion of words that represent the sounds that might appear in a scene. Students examine the different sound effects that appear in a graphic story. Invite students to interpret the words by creating the accompanying sounds. What sounds might they add to different scenes in the story?

TIMELINE

Students create a timeline of events to show what happens chronologically in the graphic story. They choose five to ten key events that would summarize the story. These events can be represented as a series of still images.

MOVIE POSTER

Students imagine that the graphic story is going to be made into a movie. They create a poster including words and pictures to advertise the movie. Students can improvise a sales-pitch meeting, in which the author/artist of a graphic novel needs to convince one or more producers to create a film version of the movie.

MOVIE TRAILERS

Media Connections

Bitstripsforschool.com
Brainpopjr.com
Comic Life

A number of graphic stories have been made into movies. Students can choose a favorite graphic story that they think would make an entertaining movie. In groups, students create a movie trailer by improvising one (or more) scenes that would serve as a preview of the movie.

VIDEOTAPE

Once students have prepared a readers theatre or improvised version of a graphic story, the presentation can be videotaped for others to watch.

Script Variation: From Graphic Page to Script

Demonstrate how a graphic text can be transformed into a script text using an example from a source that the students have met.

If students have been assigned different pages from a graphic novel, they can present a play version by showing each scene in turn. To begin, this could be just one or two pages of the script. Alternatively, some graphic novels are written in chapters and students can work to prepare a script for that chapter.

1. Assign students an excerpt from a graphic novel. Have students consider the use of narration, the number of characters speaking, and what they are saying or thinking.
   - Narrative captions can be assigned to the role of narrator or narrators.
   - It is not necessary to copy all the words that appear on the pages. Students should be invited to add or eliminate dialogue as they see fit.
2. Challenge students to add stage directions by explaining how the actors might say their lines and suggesting an action or movement they might include.
3. One or more students can be the transcriber for this activity, as the group negotiates the written script. It is best to have a word-processed copy that can be duplicated for others to read.
4. Once students have completed the written script, they can assume the role of the characters and rehearse an interpretation of the scene(s). Students should have an opportunity to practice each of the different roles.
5. (optional) Groups can exchange scripts so that each group interprets and rehearses the scripts that others have written. Partnered groups can share their work with each other and "direct" the scenes that they have written.
6. Once students are familiar with the script through repeated rehearsal, encourage them to present the scene that they have prepared.
7. The script can be rehearsed and presented into a polished play presentation. Decisions about costumes, props, transitions, and music can be considered for a final presentation to share with an audience.

The following example is a scripted version based on an excerpt from the graphic novel *Persepolis: The story of a childhood* by Marjane Satrapi (see page 83).

NARRATOR: The hotel room in Madrid. Getting ready to return home.

NARRATOR #2: The TV showed a map of Iran and a black cloud covering the country little by little.

MOTHER: What in the world is this?

FATHER: Too bad we don't understand Spanish.

MOTHER: Maybe they're talking about pollution.

MARJANE: Isn't Tehran the fourth most polluted city in the world?

FATHER: It looks like we're talking about the whole country, not just the capital.

NARRATOR: The next day my grandmother picked us up at the airport.

MARJANE: Grandma. I got you a present. It's a black dress.

NARRATOR: She looked worried.

MOTHER: Mother, is everything all right.

GRANDMOTHER: Yes…

MOTHER: It's good to be back. There's no place like home.

GRANDMOTHER: True. But soon there will be no home.

FATHER: Why do you say that?

GRANDMOTHER: Haven't you heard?

MARJANE: Haven't heard what?

GRANDMOTHER: We're at war!

FATHER, MOTHER, MARJANE: WHAT!?

Extensions

- Students retell the story in tableau images.

- Students write a narrative caption that they think might have accompanied each illustration. Captions can be written in first person to give the image a role perspective.
- Have students prepare an improvisation that would tell the story that they have created. Which characters will be in the scene? What will they say?
- Single images can be divided amongst different groups. Each group can prepare a story based on their picture. Rehearsed improvisations can be shared with others. Scenes can be presented sequentially to create a short play.
- Students create an illustration that they think might appear before or after one of the images they have been working with.

Assessment: Focus on Communication

Name: _____ Date: _____

Does the student...	Consistently	Sometimes	Not Yet
• Reveal thoughts willingly	☐	☐	☐
• Explain and describe ideas clearly	☐	☐	☐
• Share personal connections and experiences	☐	☐	☐
• Accept and build on the ideas as of others	☐	☐	☐
• Make positive suggestions to complete tasks and build the drama	☐	☐	☐
• Raise significant questions	☐	☐	☐
• Communicate ideas through art, movement and/or writing	☐	☐	☐
• Communicate thoughtfully in role	☐	☐	☐
• Revise and rehearse to interpret and present text out loud	☐	☐	☐
• Seem to enjoy exploring texts, (e.g., graphic novels and comics)	☐	☐	☐

Comments

Pembroke Publishers ©2010 *Drama Schemes, Themes & Dreams* by Larry Swartz and Debbie Nyman ISBN 978-1-55138-253-1

Journey to Freedom

> Opportunities for reflection following work in drama are critical in helping students understand how difficult life is for many people and how vital it is to advocate for everyone's place in history, for their voice in the present, and for their imprint on the future.
>
> — from *Teaching Fairly in an Unfair World* by Kathy Gould Lundy (2008: 55)

Drama Theme: History

I do not live in the past, but the past lives in me.
—Elie Wiesel, Spirit of Hope Celebration, Toronto, May 31, 2010

People like to tell stories of journeys, whether that journey is one that happened only a few steps away or across the continents. We often tell stories of local outings, vacations. or adventures, and many families like to tell stories of the journey of their ancestors and how they came to be where they are. Through stories we can began to understand what happened before we were born. Stories help to make us feel part of the history of a people. To understand the past is to know the future. Every culture has a story from the past of a journey fuelled with the hopes of a better life, sometimes out of choice, sometimes out of necessity. The movement of the African American experience from slavery to freedom is one possible path of this drama structure. This drama theme considers the universal plight and challenges of anyone who has had to flee. Students can tell their own stories of journeys and connect them to the stories of others in order to better understand the human need to be free.

LEARNING OPPORTUNITIES

- To explore the concept of journey through movement, visual arts, and story-telling
- To communicate ideas, narratives, and dreams through the physical self using dance techniques
- To share personal stories and tell stories in role about journeys
- To experience verbatim theatre by interpreting first-person accounts; and to plan, develop, and present authentic narratives gathered through primary research
- To use prior knowledge and gather research about the Underground Railroad experience
- To identify, negotiate, and solve problems in role
- To understand how to trust others and to ask for help in order to survive freely

- To examine a historical event through a variety of perspectives
- To investigate how to secure and protect rights and freedoms in today's world

Launching the Drama: Focus on Movement

1. SEPARATE AND ATTACH

- Students walk randomly in the room.
- When you call out, "Attach," students beside one another attach to each other in pairs or small groups and continue walking in any configuration. Students can attach in groups of varying numbers, e.g. attach to two other people, four other people, etc.
- When you call, "Separate," students scatter.
- As the activity continues, students can move in different ways: slow motion, hopping, skipping, jogging, giant steps, spinning, etc.

2. MY MOVEMENT MAP

- Students are each given a blank piece of paper. They are invited to create a quick non-figurative sketch that fills the page. The image can include lines, shapes, dots, etc.
- Challenge the students to use this drawing as a movement map. Students work independently to move about the room, interpreting their drawings. In what ways might they move according to the lines and shapes they've created? How might they begin and end their movement piece? Encourage students to practice the movement pattern in a variety of ways.
- Students exchange maps and try to interpret a friend's movement map.

Extensions

a) Students work in pairs and join maps together to create a movement piece using images from their illustrations.
b) The activity can be repeated by having the students work in groups of four. Students create a movement piece that weaves together movements from each person's map. Have the students consider the following:
  - How will they begin and end the piece?
  - What movements will be repeated?
  - What patterns can they incorporate into their choreography?
  - What movements will be done independently? In unison?
  - How might the movement piece change when music is added?

c) The students can use their movement maps to create sound images or soundscapes. Instead of moving to the map, the students make sounds using their voices, hands, or feet.

3. CIRCUIT RELAY

- Students line up in teams of five. Each team designs and draws a map of a route or circuit, marking four stops on the route; e.g., stopping to touch a wall or a window.

- At your signal, the first person in line runs the circuit and returns to the team, at which point the second person joins the first person and they run the route together.
- Repeat this until all five members have run the route joined together.

4. POWER OF THE HAND

- Students work in pairs facing each other. Each places one hand palm-forward close to, but not touching, the partner's opposite hand.
- One person is the designated leader, who has the power in their hand to lead the other student through the space. The follower must work hard to stay close but not touch hands.
- Encourage students to use different levels, change direction and speed, and cover the entire area of the space.
- Have students repeat the activity after changing leaders.
- While students are moving, call out, "Freeze," and students freeze, maintaining their positions. Encourage students to look around the room and observe the use of levels, focus, and physical arrangements.

Extensions

a) Have students make a tiny physical connection (e.g., at pinky fingers or wrists) and continue the exercise; first with eyes open, and then, if students are comfortable with each other, closing their eyes for a few moments.
b) Have students continue the activity in small and large groups. Encourage the students to use both abstract and concrete movements.

Reflection

- How did it feel to have the power? How did it feel to be the follower with no power?
- What did you do to make your partner feel comfortable enough to work with eyes closed? How did your partner make you feel comfortable enough to close your eyes?
- How did you feel moving with your eyes closed?
- Describe an incident in the real world that you were reminded of when working in this activity.

5. RUBBER CHICKEN

- Students stand in a circle.
- Everyone shakes their right hands up in the air eight times, while counting out quickly, "1, 2, 3, 4, 5, 6, 7, 8."
- Encourage students to make the counting fast and loud, and the shaking energetic.
- The activity continues with left hand, then right leg, then left leg.
- As soon as all four limbs have been introduced counting from 1 to 8, repeat shaking and counting from 1 to 7, then 1 to 6, and so on, until you finally shake each limb once, counting, "1" as you shake it.
- Everyone then shouts out, "Rubber chicken!" and shakes the whole body like a rubber chicken.

Note: The addition of slow, strong instrumental music will support the students as they work through the exercise.

- Students work in pairs. Partner A begins by freezing into a position that fills as much space as possible (e.g. arms spread wide, legs pointing forward) and then freezes.
- Partner B must then assume a position that fills in the space that partner A has left. Partner B freezes into this position.
- Partner A unfreezes and tries to connect himself or herself to partner B, by filling in the space.
- Continue the exercise until the students are comfortable with it.
- Repeat the activity in groups of four or five. Each student is given a number and freezes into position when you call out that number. Each student decides on his or her own when to unfreeze.
- In the activity, there is always one student moving and the others still. Encourage the students to focus on the transition movement from one position to the next. Encourage them to move smoothly and economically, and in silence, from position to position.
- Introduce a word or phrase to the students to motivate and inform the transition movement and the frozen shapes they create. Each group receives a different but related word: e.g., the seasons, different elements, natural phenomena. Ask the students not to share their words with other groups. For the purposes of this theme, students can explore words connected to the journey experience; e.g., *escape, trapped, lost, liberated, adventure, arrival, safety*.
- Groups continue to work in the same process, motivated by the word.
- After some practice time, half of the groups observe the other half as they work. The observing groups record on chart paper the words, phrases, and sounds that they thought about while observing the work.
- Continue the process with the other half observing and recording.

Extension: Vocal exploration

Students explore different ways of vocally expressing the collected words. Read the words aloud: whispering, echoing, shouting, singing, chanting, changing tone and pace. Students then decide on an order for the words and assign specific parts. Students create two whole-class presentations: in each presentation, half the class reads and presents the words while the other half works through the filling-in-the-spaces activity. Using this process with specifically chosen words— e.g., *war, peace, conflict*, etc.—could lead to a performance for a specific occasion such as Remembrance Day.

Reflection

- How did the work change when you added a specific word to the exercise?
- Describe a moment that you thought was particularly effective and explain why it was effective.
- Which role did you prefer, the movement or choral, and why?
- What have you learned about journeys from this activity?

Moving Freely

by Lorraine Sutherns, instructional leader, Drama and Dance,
Toronto District School Board

To dance is to be out of yourself. Larger, more beautiful, more powerful.
—Agnes De Mille

As someone who works with teachers who are looking for ways to engage students in dance, I have found success in cultivating dance explorations within the context of drama. It allows the students to explore the space between the words, to pause, expand, crystallize, and deepen the meaning of the drama through movement. The world of drama embodies our collective experience and gives students a rich context from which to enter into the dance work. Whether they are creating dance phrases from the perspective of themselves or from a character in the drama, a kinesthetic interpretation allows them to explore the themes and issues on a deeper level.

Moving into teenagehood can be a tough time to approach dance. For students (and teachers), self-consciousness, body image, strong ideas about what dance is and is not, together with deep perceptions of themselves as being "good or not good at dancing,"—all this prevents them from moving freely.

What is beauty? What does it look like? Who and what define it? Where do we find it? These questions framed a recent drama dance exploration with a Grade 8 class. Together we explored the concept of beauty from the perspective of a central character who is searching for beauty in a world that seems cold, disconnected, and unfair. The source was the picture book *Something Beautiful* by Sharon Dennis Wyeth, and the students were immediately drawn into and inspired by the themes of the story.

In the drama work, they created still images of what they imagined the character saw as she walked through her community. They created scenes of her conversations with people when she asked them these questions: "What does beauty mean to you?" "How do you hold onto your vision in spite of the challenges facing you?" "Where could I, myself, go to find it?" Through writing in role from different perspectives, the community gave advice to the young girl as she moved along on her quest to find her "something beautiful."

After exploring the character's journey, students consolidated their learning by responding to these questions: *What does beauty mean to you? What is the shape of beauty? Where do you find beauty in your own life?*

The rich imagery from which they developed powerful dance phrases came from their written responses. They wrote, "I find beauty…"

- in the awakening of my senses
- in the voices of people around me
- deep within my soul
- in every corner of my community
- in endless possibilities
- in the hazy pink-purple glow of sunsets
- in the infinite everlasting shape of a circle
- in the pride and respect I have for myself
- in the essence of the earth

The personal connections students made to the story were particularly moving when they engaged in a dance activity that was inspired by this writing. In groups of five, students chose an image from their writing and used it to develop one strong movement. The students were numbered 1 to 5. The groups were mixed so that new groups included a student from each of the former groups and five distinct movements from which to work with.

They worked as choreographers, sequencing the movements together and focusing on transitions, timing, and tempo. Each group worked to make choices that would enhance their collective interpretations of beauty. They decided where they would place themselves in relation to one another and experimented with diagonals, circles, random facings, solos, duets, groups, corridors, and staggered lines.

The students then wove the dances back into the drama context by sharing them as a dream sequence. Each dance began as the teacher, in role as the girl, circled around the space, igniting the dances one by one, representing her hopes and emerging vision of beauty.

Exploring dance within the context of drama allowed these students to kinesthetically embrace and internalize their existing perceptions of beauty, and then project a new and deeper understanding of what beauty means to them.

Dance within Drama: A Few Tips

1. Don't overwhelm with too many words or ideas to dance about. Less is more. Start with simple action words, prepositional phrases, and brief poetic segments to inspire the movement.
2. Have students create short bursts of movement. Play with the order, timing, space, and quality of movements as well as repetition of key motifs.
3. Side-coach students with simple questions based on the elements of dance: Body, Energy, Space, Time, Relationship. (e.g. *What happens if you slow down your gesture and move forward through space at the same time?*)
4. Once movement phrases have been created, invite students to experiment with interesting spatial formations, relationships, and arrangements to build visual interest, depth, and design. Circles, lines, random scattering, V-shapes, solos, duets, small and large groups, different facings, etc. are all visually stunning and powerful.
5. Weave the dance creations into the drama, sharing them with spoken word, choral readings, monologues, etc.

Framing the Theme: The Journey

CREATING A MURAL

Find the cost of freedom,
buried in the ground,
Mother Earth will swallow you
Lay your body down.
— *Find the Cost of Freedom* by Crosby, Stills, Nash

Invite students to the mural paper to brainstorm the word "journey" considering the following:

- What is a journey?
- How do you feel when you prepare for a journey?
- How would you express or draw "journey"? What are some places in the world you would like to journey to?
- Record words, phrases, images that come to mind when you think about the previous activities and the journeys referred to in the movement work.
- Record a word or phrase that comes to your mind when you read other people's words on the mural.
- What color marker would best express your words?
- Can you connect some of the words with other words, or lines or drawings?

Inform the students that they will continue to fill the mural with words, phrases, and images as the drama unfolds.

PERSONAL JOURNEY STORIES

Upon completion of the activities that follow, invite the students back to the mural to add new words, phrases, and images that express their new learning of "journey" acquired through the activities.

Have students work in pairs for a Think–Pair–Share activity on the topic of journeys. The following prompts can be used to tell a story from their own lives, or about someone they know:

- Getting lost
- A great vacation
- A school excursion
- Leaving was difficult
- A safe arrival

This storytelling activity can be done in a double-circle format with the group in two circles, and A and B pairs facing each other. After each brief story, one circle moves one or two people to the right so that each student faces a new partner. This can be repeated each time in different variations.

See Tic-Tac-Tale Chart on page 97.

TIC-TAC-TALE

A chart (see page 97) is given to each group of three or four students. The students are told to select any three items that appear in a row (as if they were playing Tic-Tac-Toe). Once the group has negotiated and decided which vertical, horizontal, or diagonal row they will explore, they invent a story that includes those items in some way. After the story has been invented, students dramatize the story using one or more of the following: tableau, narration, improvisation, mime, movement, story theatre.

Extensions

The following activities are alternative strategies for using the Tic-Tac-Tale Chart in a variety of group situations

a) Students create a tableau play to show the beginning, middle, and end of a journey story.
b) Students choose two rows to build a story
c) Each person in the group adds one sentence to build a continuous story; the group has two minutes to complete the story. The activity can be repeated by telling the story in role.
d) Create a chart with new words or phrases.
e) Students use their invented stories as stimuli for writing.

Strategy Scheme: Teacher in Role

TEACHER WORKING IN ROLE INSIDE THE DRAMA

Teachers work in role to…

Students will observe you in role, which maybe the only example they have of role play.
—Cecily O'Neill, *Drama Worlds* (1995: 99)

Model authentic role-playing

Many students are new to drama and to working authentically in role. They come to class with pre-conceived notions of what drama and acting are about. The students observe the teacher working thoughtfully in role, listening and speaking in role, interacting with students. In this way, the students begin to understand the expectations of role-play, the appropriate behaviors of role play, and the power of role-play to shape the drama, to express and communicate ideas.

Activate the drama

The teacher can step into a particular role in a particular context and immediately activate and set the drama in motion. In role, the teacher can provide details of the context and the world, and endow students with a particular role. In role, the teacher can set the mood and create a sense of excitement and urgency for entering into this world. See Ways to Begin Drama with Teacher in Role on page 99.

Tic-Tac-Tale Chart

An old suitcase	A bridge	Mountain pass
A key	Border crossing with guards	A crumpled map
Deer	A passport	A raft

Pembroke Publishers ©2010 *Drama Schemes, Themes & Dreams* by Larry Swartz and Debbie Nyman ISBN 978-1-55138-253-1

Heighten tension and deepen commitment

At every step of the process, the teacher can step inside the drama in role to re-ignite the tension and deepen engagement and commitment. The teacher can take on a new role with new information that will re-focus the students and challenge them to see another perspective, another implication of their choices in the drama.

Build the narrative, move the drama forward

The teacher in role can bring new information to the drama, can move the drama forward into the future to develop the story or into the past to build the backstory of the drama. Working in role will bring new purpose to the development of the narrative.

Manage the learning and behaviors

The teacher can select roles to manage the classroom challenges and behaviors of students. The teacher can select roles that will bring purpose to certain behaviors. In role and inside the drama, the teacher can give students reasons for listening, for silence, for attention and concentration, and most importantly for respect.

Consolidate and reflect

The teacher can select and create roles near the conclusion of the drama to model and encourage deep reflection. The teacher can reflect, summarize, challenge, and guide the students to reflect in role as well.

Some of the examples within this chart are found within the Drama Structure that starts on page 100. Other examples could be used within a similar structure.

Purpose	Roles	Examples
Activate the drama by setting the context, endowing students with role	One who needs help	• "I am leaving tonight after dark. I know I could be caught and killed but I cannot stay here any longer. I will need your help. Do you have any advice for me? Is there anything I should bring? Will any of you come with me?"
Heighten the tension, set the tone, deepen commitment	One who brings information that will alter the situation, bring another perspective (new character); messenger	• "We know you have been hiding in the forest. You have been seen and so there are people who know you are out there. I have a message for you." • "We must work quickly and quietly. We do not know how long we will be able to meet. We are all in danger."
Build the narrative, move the drama forward	Leader, facilitator, one of the group	• "We have been traveling for two weeks now. We are tired and some of us are ill. I do not think we can continue on this way. What do you want to do?" • "We need to make a plan. Should we ask for help from the outside?"
Manage the learning and behaviors from within, giving purpose to the work	Leader, facilitator	• "We must listen to the stories so that we can pass them on should any of us not make it to freedom." • "We must agree to certain conditions for the meeting." • "Who will speak first? What exactly will we ask for? How shall we arrange the room?"
Consolidate and reflect	One who is the outsider, who does not know the story; a newcomer or an ancestor	• "My grandparents made this journey through the underground railroad. What can you tell me about it?"

Not only is the teacher engaged in an active process of striving to see with the children's eyes, but they must also see each child through a professional lens, and, at the same time, shape the whole collective experience.

—Maggie Hulson, *Schemes for Classroom Drama* (2006: 5)

Teacher in role of documentary director/producer interviewing students, in role as high-performance Olympic athletes, for a documentary on people who strive for excellence. How do they train? How do they motivate themselves? What qualities lead them to excellence?
Purpose: to build belief in the context; to deepen understanding

Teacher in role as the nanny to the princess has called together the students in role as other servants and workers in the castle. The princess has fallen asleep and cannot be awakened. The nanny has tried many safe ways and now she is especially worried because the king and queen are expected back from their journey. They will want to see the princess right away.
Purpose: to set the context and develop a sense of urgency; to encourage a variety of possibilities

Teacher in role of animal behaviorist biologist comes to students, in role as villagers, to collect stories about wolves. There have been stories coming out of this village about wolves behaving in unusual ways, e.g., chasing children in the forest, etc. What do you know about this?
Purpose: to encourage the students to view the story from a new perspective, summarize the story by retelling with a purpose

Teacher in role of the head of a communications centre in the future speaks to students, in role as communication experts, to decide how to proceed, what action to take. At this point in the world, we have been communicating with many different planets and this evening we received a message from a planet called Narvis: *Our planet is dying…please help…Our planet is dying.*
Purpose: to build context; to endow students with role and responsibility; to focus students

Teacher in role of spy for a medieval community has called a secret meeting in the night to inform students, in role as villagers, about a decree from the king. The decree states that knights will be using the villagers' fields for preparing for tournaments. They will arrive in the morning with the horses, jousting equipment, and weapons. What shall we do to prepare, to be ready for them?
Purpose: to inform; to build context; to create mood and atmosphere; to set the story in motion

Teacher in role of one of a group of travelers comes to the students, in role as fellow travelers, and explains that she has stumbled upon a village with a special secret. This village has a well with water that will give eternal life. The traveler wants to drink the water but also wants her fellow travelers to drink with her.
Purpose: to set the context; to challenge the students to explore the implications and consequences of choice

Teacher in role of the woodsman, who has been instructed by the queen to bring her the heart of Snow White, comes to the students, in role as other servants to the queen, seeking advice on what to do as he feels that he cannot follow her orders.
Purpose: to set the context; to challenge students to explore implications and consequences, and devise a plan to set the drama in motion

Teacher in role of recruiting officer for a time-travel mission meets with the students, in role as recruiters, to create the criteria for choosing the time traveler.

History is a symphony of echoes heard and unheard. It is a poem with events as verses.

—Charles Angoff, author

How will the chosen individual travel in time? Will he or she travel alone? Will he or she tell his/her story or is this to be kept a secret? How long will he or she be away?

Purpose: to set the drama in motion; to begin to negotiate and build the circumstances of the drama together

Teacher in role of spokesperson for the police addresses students, in role as parents, about the circumstances around the arrest of teenagers for breaking curfew. The curfew was established to counter violence in the community and, on this particular night, a significant number of teenagers broke curfew. Why did they break curfew? How did they organize? What did you notice about their behavior in the days leading up to this night?

Purpose: to convey information; to set drama in motion; to begin to develop the drama

These are merely premises, starting points for the teacher in role to invite students into the drama to take on roles, establish a context, and begin to wrestle with the implications and consequences of the situation. Teachers can continue the drama, building a structure with the students using a variety of drama strategies.

A Drama Structure Using a Visual Image

ART ALIVE: TABLEAU

See *Come Look With Me: Discovering African-American art for children* by James Haywood, Jr. (2005) for a detailed reproduction of this image.

In groups of six, students gathered around the image, shown on page 101, placed on the floor in the room. The students circled the image closely, examining it, and then considered and shared five details about the image they felt were important and five questions they had about the image. Students each chose a character to role-play in the image; in 60 seconds together they re-created the photograph, paying attention to every detail—the focus of the character, proximity to others in the image, facial expressions, props. On a cue from the teacher, one student stepped out of the image to direct students in any changes they needed to make to exactly replicate the photograph. Students then memorized their positions to be able to re-create the images.

A PICTURE IS WORTH...: ROLE PLAY

Groups re-created the images all together in a circular formation, facing into the centre of the circle so that each group could see others' images.

Half of the groups in the circle remained frozen in the tableaux; half of the groups examined the tableaux and considered the teacher's questions:

- What do you notice about the travelers?
- What do you notice about the character you played in the image now that you are outside the image?
- What do you know about their journey?
- How do you think they are feeling?

Students outside the images tapped the shoulders of students in role inside the images to describe in a word or two their feelings in that moment or what they were hoping for in that moment.

Image of Harriet Tubman

Harriet © Estate of Elizabeth Catlett, SODRAC, Montreal/VAGA, New York (2010)

The students outside the images then re-created their images and the other half of the class stepped out of role to observe as audience, again discussing what they were coming to know about the travelers. They then questioned the students inside the tableaux, who responded in role:

- Why did you choose to make this journey?
- What do you hope for at the end of the journey?
- What are you afraid of as you make this journey?

THE TRAVELERS' STORIES: STORYTELLING IN ROLE

All the students re-created their tableaux and observed the tableaux of other groups to find the students role-playing their characters. Students playing the same characters met as a new group. Together they built their stories, considering the following questions:

- Why did you choose to leave?
- What have you brought with you, in your pockets, in your clothing?
- What skills and strengths do you bring to the group?
- What are you most fearful of?
- What will you do when you arrive at your destination?

After creating the stories, the students planned how they would share the telling of their stories.

The whole class met to share the stories. The teacher, in the role of a fellow traveler, set the scene

> We have traveled through the night and we can rest now just before dawn. We will not be able to continue through the daylight in case we are seen. We left in such a hurry I thought maybe we could take a moment to tell each other a little bit of our story so that we know what each of us can do to help the group on the journey and so that if any of us do not make it, we will be able to pass on our stories.

Each group then shared their stories briefly and quietly.

ART IMAGES: ILLUSTRATING

Each group returned to the mural to draw images to represent both the place they had come from and their imaginings and dreams of their destination.

LIFE ON THE ROAD: TABLEAUX AND MOVEMENT

The students considered the travelers' lives after being on the road for several days or weeks. The students re-created the original image and froze; the teacher asked them to move in slow motion for a minute to reveal how this image might change after traveling for several days or weeks. The students worked individually and in silence briefly until the teacher asked them to freeze. The students remained in the image but observed how the images had changed. Students in their groups shared how their characters had changed both physically and emotionally.

The teacher moved the drama forward with voice-over narration:

> The travelers continued to walk in the darkness and sleep during the day but after several days they found that they had no more food, they were weary and some felt too weak to go on. They were outside a village.

Teacher in role called the travelers together, took on the role of a traveler, and addressed the group:

> I am worried that we may not be able to continue the journey. We have very little food left, we are tired and some of us do not seem strong enough to continue. We are outside of a village and I think we should seek help. I have heard that there are sympathetic people in this village who might help us. What do you think? How might we go about asking? What shall we ask for?

Students explored the possibilities of asking for help. They considered the risks they were taking in asking for help and they considered the risks the villagers would be taking in helping them. The teacher, in role as one of the travelers, challenged the students to devise a plan to seek assistance. Will one person go? Will they send a group? What should they ask for? How should they approach someone?

In the end they decided to send one group (from the tableau groups) of travelers. They prepared the group by creating a list of their needs, the essentials they would ask for, and any other important tasks the villagers could do for them. They rehearsed what they would say to the villagers to convince them to help.

The group of travelers continued to prepare while the rest of the class role-played the villagers, planning what they would say to the travelers, and brainstorming questions they would ask, how they might help them, and what they were prepared to do, given the risks.

The teacher moved from group to group, coaching and challenging the students to consider all the possibilities. When the groups were prepared, they decided where the meeting would take place and arranged the space accordingly. They decided that they would meet in the church basement after dark to avoid being seen by less-sympathetic villagers.

VOICING CONCERNS: MEETING

The teacher played the role of a villager and began the meeting, setting the tone and inviting the groups to sit across from each other.

> We need to get started. We do not know how long will we be able to meet. We are all in danger. Others who do not sympathize may have learned of our plans. We must work quickly and quietly. We will work in as little light as possible. The travelers will need to return to the forest before dawn. There is much for us to fear. Let's begin.

The two groups expressed their needs and concerns. Some villagers were reluctant to help and needed to be convinced. In the end they negotiated how the villagers would help the travelers.

WARNINGS: CORRIDOR OF VOICES

The meeting ended with the travelers leaving the meeting through a corridor of voices. The villagers formed two lines facing each other and gave advice and support or warnings to the travelers as they passed by.

REVISITING THE MURAL: REFLECTION

The students came out of role and reflected on the meeting. The teacher asked the travelers to describe how they felt both in and out of role as they traveled through the corridor. The teacher asked the students in role as villagers how they felt at the end. Did they think the travelers were strong enough to complete their journey? How had they made this possible? Were they worried at all for themselves, given that they had taken this risk?

The students returned to the mural for a last opportunity to record the journey. The teacher asked them to incorporate words or phrases that they remembered that echoed their feelings or thoughts, to incorporate their final thoughts as travelers on the journey, what they had learned through the journey.

VOICES FROM THE PAST: THOUGHT TRACKING

The students closely examined the mural. Each chose a line or phrase that spoke strongly to him or her, stood in that place, and in ten seconds created a physical image to interpret the line. When all the students were frozen, the teacher traveled through the group, tapping the students on the shoulder to signal to them to say or read the line aloud. The teacher was able to travel back to a line or student to repeat the phrase; phrases could overlap.

The students took these phrases to their journals and continued the phrase as a reflection of the work.

CULMINATING ACTIVITY: DREAMS/MOVEMENT AND DANCE DRAMA

The students returned to the home groups created in the tableau of the original photograph and discussed and imagined the dreams of the travelers many years after the journey to freedom. They brainstormed images from the journey that might represent both the challenges and rewards, both their fear and courage. How could these dreams tell their stories to their children, grandchildren, and communities?

The teacher reviewed the movement activities and exercises from the previous lessons—My Movement Map (page 91), Power of the Hand (page 92), Fill in the Spaces (page 93)—to incorporate into the piece. The teacher reminded the students that dreams are fluid, ever-changing, and often symbolic and otherworldly. The teacher selected appropriate music (instrumental, new age) to play while the students were rehearsing and performing.

The dreams began with the students in the original tableau and ended in a new and powerful tableau. The mural became a backdrop for the performances. The dreams were presented one after the other seamlessly in the original circle where students shared the original tableaux.

Reflection

The students reflected on the performances, discussing both the theatrical successes and their feelings about what they witnessed. In discussing the performance elements they commented on the following questions:

- What moment was particularly effective in the piece and why?
- Describe an image that stands out for you.
- How did the music help you to perform?
- Were there any recurring images in the dreams? Why do you think this happened?

Extending the Drama

FINDING FREEDOM VOICES OF TODAY

Invite the students to interview friends and/or family who have either experienced or know the stories of ancestors who might have experienced a journey to freedom. The stories could be shaped into monologues and presented to the class.

UNDERGROUND RAILROAD

Students can research the Underground Railroad to learn about the signs, the abolitionists, the network, and the organizations that assisted people on their journey to freedom.

A FREEDOM DOCUMENTARY

Invite students to imagine that they are creating a collection of stories for a freedom display or installation to travel around the world. The stories could come from different parts of the world, and would include art, poetry, photographs, recorded voices, and images.

MUSIC OF FREEDOM

Songs have played an important role as people sought freedom throughout history. Invite students to research and listen to freedom songs and then write their own freedom raps, songs, and chants.

FREEDOM COLLAGE

Invite students to create collages, using print images or computer technology and graphics, that depict their concept of freedom. They can select music or a song to enrich the collage. They can e-mail collages to students or share in the classroom. Students explain and justify their choices of images and the organization of the images.

When every heart joins every
    heart and together yearns for
    liberty,
That's when we'll be free.
When every hand joins every
    hand and together molds our
    destiny,
That's when we'll be free
— from *Hymn to Freedom* by Oscar
Peterson

MY FREEDOM AND RIGHTS

Students work in groups and make a list of their personal freedoms and rights in this school community, in the world. Ask students to order the rights from the most important to the least important.

THE RIGHTS AND FREEDOMS OF THE CHILD CONVENTION: WHOLE-CLASS ROLE PLAY

In the role of the chair of an International Conference for Children's Rights and Freedoms, call together the students, in the role of conference delegates, to put together a Charter of Rights and Freedoms for all children around the world. Explain to the delegates:

> You have been called here today to put together a Charter of Children's Rights and Freedoms. Children are particularly vulnerable. Children have different needs than adults; therefore we need to develop a Charter specifically for children that will protect all children. We are asking you to list eight important rights that all countries can agree to uphold. Do you have any questions?

You can answer some of the students' questions and then divide them into groups to decide on eight recommendations. Students come back to the whole-class group and report their recommendations. Students negotiate together and create one Charter for Children's Rights and Freedoms.

Extensions

Students can

a) write a report to the conference committee defending their number-one recommendation
b) write their own Freedom for Children poems
c) create, share, and defend a new logo for Children's Rights: a sign, gesture, drawing.

Script Variation: Monologue

See page 107 for Freedom Voices.

1. Provide each student a copy of one of the narratives. Ask the students to read the excerpt alone.
2. Students read the piece aloud twice while walking through the space.
3. Students seek out a partner with a different excerpt and partners read their pieces to each other while walking through the space.
4. In pairs, students exchange their selections and listen, with eyes closed, to their pieces read aloud by their partners. Following the reading and listening, ask the students to share with their partners what they learned about the person by listening to the story read to them.
5. Invite students to find the other students in the room with the same selection and form a group.
6. Working in groups, students discuss and record three things they know for sure about the speaker of the piece and three things they would like to know.
7. Students then underline or highlight what they feel are the three most important words in the piece. Invite students to share and defend their choices.

Freedom Voices

William Johnson

I had grown up quite large before I thought anything about liberty. The fear of being sold south had more influence in inducing me to leave than any other thing. Master used to say that if we didn't suit him he would put us in his pocket quick—meaning he would sell us. My feet were frostbitten on my way north but I would rather have died on the way than go back. I have been trying to learn to read since I came here, and I know a great many fugitives who are trying to learn.

Harriet Tubman

I grew up like a neglected weed—ignorant of liberty having no experience of it. Then I was not happy or contented. Every time I saw a white man I was afraid of being carried away. I had two sisters carried away in a chain gang—one of them left two children. We were always uneasy. Now I've been free I know what a dreadful condition slavery is. I have seen hundreds of escaped slaves, but I never saw one who was willing to go back and be a slave. I have no opportunity to see my friends in my native land. We would rather stay in our native land if we could be as free there as we are here. I think slavery is the next thing to hell. If a person would send another person into bondage, he would, it appears to me, to be bad enough to send him into hell, if he could.

Mrs. James Seward

The slaves want to get away bad enough. I am from the eastern shore of Maryland. I was never sent to school, nor allowed to go to church. We were all afraid of master, of the beatings, of the cruelty. When I saw him coming my heart would jump into my mouth, as if I had seen a serpent. I have been waiting to come away for eight years back. I waited for Jim Seward to get ready. Jim had promised to take me away and marry me. Our master would allow no marriages on the farm. When Jim had got ready he let me know—he brought me two suits of clothes—men's clothes which he had bought on purpose for me to disguise myself. I put on both suits to keep me warm. We eluded pursuit and reached Canada in safety.

Mrs. Ellis

It is more than a year that I left slavery in Delaware, having been thirty-two years a slave. I was brought up in ignorance. I felt put down—oppressed in spirit. I have had four children—two died there and two I have brought with me. My master threatened to sell me and keep my children and I left. I got off without much trouble. I suffered a great deal from wet and cold, on the first part of the way—afterwards I was helped by kind white men. I can't forget it. I sometimes dream that I am pursued, and when I wake, I am almost scared to death.

William Grose

After my wife was gone, I felt very uneasy. At length, I picked up spunk, and said I would start. All this time, I dreamed on nights that I was getting clear. This put the notion into my head to start—a dream that I had reached a free soil and was perfectly safe. Sometimes I felt as if I would get clear, and again as if I would not. I had many doubts and fears. I said to myself—I recollect it well—I can't die but once; if they catch me, they can kill me: I'll defend myself as far as I can. I armed myself with an old razor and made a start, alone, telling no one, not even my brother. All the way along, I felt dread—a heavy load on me all the way. I found a friend who helped me on the way to Canada.

I served twenty-five years in slavery and about five I have been free. I feel now like a man.

Pembroke Publishers ©2010 *Drama Schemes, Themes & Dreams* by Larry Swartz and Debbie Nyman ISBN 978-1-55138-253-1

8. Students select one word and create a physical position to represent the word. Ask the groups to build one image in their groups by connecting the words and physical shapes.

9. Students sit in a circle with their groups. One person begins to read aloud the passage. He or she reads only one line. The activity continues as the lines of text are read consecutively. It is important to have the students proceed through the passage more than once, so that each student experiences different lines.

10. Ask the students to create a group reading of the piece. Direct them to use a variety of voices; e.g. solo lines, small groups, and lines or words said as a whole group. Direct them to create an image of the character to be in while reading.

11. Provide the students with time to rehearse and decide if they will memorize their lines or read them.

12. You can decide an order for the narratives; or the students can share their readings in a random order, and then the teacher and students can negotiate an order to effectively share the narratives in a theatre piece. Teacher and students might also want to give the piece a title and opening and closing lines. Other techniques to experiment with might include blending two pieces together or creating movement in between.

VERBATIM THEATRE

FreedomVoices on page 107 are authentic refugee stories that have been transcribed verbatim.

In verbatim theatre, the actual words of real people are brought to life on the stage. Unlike docudrama, students are responsible for transcribing and bringing to life the words verbatim (i.e., in their exact and original form). Actors take on the characters of the real individuals whose words are being said. In creating verbatim theatre, directors, actors, and writers agree to bring honor and integrity to the words and real people, not to misrepresent for dramatic purpose. The teacher and students can use the real words of fugitive slaves in Canada and the following exercises to begin to explore the genre of verbatim theatre. Following this exploration, the students might choose to interview family and/or friends to learn of stories of journeys to freedom in other contexts, and to transcribe the stories to create a piece of verbatim theatre.

Strategy Scheme: From Personal Voice to Theatre

1. Choosing a Topic: Although verbatim theatre can be built on an issue or theme that interests students (relationships, working), it is best when it considers an event in time that is current and relevant to their school or local community: e.g., sports event, environment or political issue, an accident, a demolition.

2. Who's Involved: Students brainstorm a list of people who had a connection to the event, or perhaps were expert on the event.

3. Building Questions: Students prepare a list of questions that need to be considered in interviewing other characters.

4. Conducting the Interviews: Students can conduct interviews independently or with friends. For best results, interviews should be audio-recorded with the permission of the participants. Alternatively, students can record the dialogue as spoken.

5. Transcribing the Conversations: A transcription is a written copy of an oral conversation. It is important to write the words as accurately as possible. To be as authentic as possible, consideration should be given to punctuation, pauses, and any utterances. This transcription becomes a working script for the students to interpret.

6. Lifting the Words from the Page: Students make decisions about how the text should be said out loud. As they work through the process, students can edit the writing, keeping parts that they think are most significant. Students need to be reminded that they cannot change the words. Students can portray the characters of the people they interviewed. Alternatively, students can pass their text on to someone else.

7. Rehearsing the Monologues: Students practice and rehearse their verbatim monologues. What voice will best give meaning to the text? What gestures will they add? How will they sit, stand, or move?

8. Sharing their Work: Each person shares his or her work. As audience members, students can make suggestions and "direct" each other's presentations.

9. Preparing to Perform: Students make decisions about the order of scenes. How might music, props, costumes, lighting, and set enrich the presentation? Students rehearse the work.

10. The Verbatim Performance: Once prepared, students choose an audience in the school to share their work with.

Monica Prendergast and Juliana Saxton (2010) have edited *Applied Theatre*, a significant collection of articles designed to help practitioners and their students consider possibilities for their own community-based theatre projects.

Drama in the Community

by Carolee Mason, drama instructor, OISE/UT

Community Partnership with Crimestoppers and the Ontario Provincial Police (OPP) was a final project introduced to the Grade 10 drama class. This initiative was intended to involve the students in developing characters through improvisation, then scripting and shooting a 20-minute film, in collaboration with the Grade 10 media arts class.

We launched the project as we had all our other units of work, with a circle discussion around the goals of the final product. In this case, I invited our OPP liaison officer to the class to explain how Crimestoppers and the police wanted to involve us in developing an educational tool for use in schools. They hoped that we could create a dramatization around youth involvement with illegal firearms.

Our liaison officer provided the "hook" for the project and promptly arrested the students' attention. We were introduced to two constables and an arsenal of decommissioned training weapons—both handguns and long guns—for the students to see, touch, and ask questions about. As well, students were provided with statistics and case studies around illegal trade in firearms across the province.

Once we learned about the challenges the illegal activity was presenting to our community and others, we launched into a period of discussion around the differences between what we understood from our liaison officer and the representation of gun culture in popular culture. If we were to create a dramatic piece to help raise awareness with other students, how could we explore the issue authentically, without sensationalism or melodrama? What did we need to learn about in order to undertake this work? We found some answers in talking further with police, Crimestoppers representatives, and film experts. As well, we examined articles from the media about gun crime across the province. We learned that, far from being an infrequent or exotic offence, violations involving firearms took place often, usually involving theft from collectors in our area. We learned that, in order to communicate our discoveries with other students through dramatization, we would need to learn to develop complex characters, script authentic dialogue, and create truthful scenes with legitimate conflict.

The students' subsequent drama work over three weeks involved a range of strategies including

- additional research
- improvised dialogue
- writing in role

- improvised scene work
- scripted scene work
- scripting
- editing and redrafting
- rehearsal
- on-set work and filming

Initially, students worked in pairs to improvise dialogue around a given dilemma. For example, using the technique of inside/outside circles, students in pairs responded to a given scenario in response to an opening line or an assigned objective: e.g., you are a principal who is asking a student to open his locker because you are suspicious about what is being hidden there/You are a parent who has just discovered your son or daughter has charged something illegal to your credit card/Two friends are deciding how to spend their paycheque and one of them wants to buy a firearm for protection. Conversations were kept brief, at no more than two or three minutes. At the conclusion of the conversation, the students in the outer circle shifted one place, meeting a new partner and repeating the process with a different opening line and new objectives. These were provided by the teacher, and revolved around moral and ethical choices.

Another subsequent lesson invited students to invent a character, based on examples from new stories. In role as one of the characters in the social circle, or as a student charged with a crime involving a break and enter, students wrote brief diary entries, e-mails, or Facebook posts. These pieces were shared in small groups. The students used their writing to invent characters and a conflict upon which they built a series of tableaux. Using a "voices in the head" strategy, the inner thoughts of each member of the tableau were heard. After sharing their work with the rest of the class as audience, students returned to groups to further develop their characters through created biographies. Working in pairs, they helped one another edit for consistency and authenticity in voice. More than anything, students wanted to avoid what they called "cheesy teen angst."

Working through all of the material, the class appointed writers, and their teacher put together a draft script that centred on a group of students socializing on a Friday night. In addition to the objective of examining illegal weapons, other events around dishonesty, intimidation, relationships, and underage drinking emerged in the narrative. After readings, scene work, and redrafting, a script was submitted to the film class and roles were cast from the Grade 10 class.

For this Collective Creation activity, students chose from a number of assigned roles. Some assumed responsibilities as lead actors, understudies, extras, and crew members. Those who elected to work on the technical side collaborated with students from the communications technology class to plan lighting, find costumes, scout locations, and establish the filming schedule. Ultimately, everyone experienced genuine collaboration in a real context. The product, a DVD production entitled *Intervention*, was shared nationally and internationally as part of a Crimestoppers of Ontario education initiative.

Assessment: Movement Rubric

	Level 1	Level 2	Level 3	Level 4
Knowledge • knowledge of movement techniques and exercises and skills	Demonstrates limited knowledge of movement strategies and techniques.	Demonstrates some knowledge of movement strategies and techniques.	Demonstrates considerable knowledge of movement strategies and techniques.	Demonstrates thorough knowledge of movement strategies and techniques.
Thinking • interpretation of ideas and feelings	Demonstrates limited ability to interpret ideas and translate into movement.	Demonstrates some ability to interpret ideas and translate into movement.	Demonstrates considerable ability to interpret ideas and translate into movement.	Demonstrates well-developed ability to interpret ideas and translate into movement.
• use of planning and processing skills in the creation of the piece (interprets, revises, edits, refines, rehearses)	Uses skills with limited effectiveness.	Uses skills with some effectiveness.	Uses skills with considerable effectiveness.	Uses skills with a high degree of effectiveness.
Communication • uses movement to communicate and represent ideas and feelings with clarity and organization	Communicates ideas and feelings with limited clarity and effectiveness.	Communicates ideas and feelings with some clarity and effectiveness.	Clearly and effectively communicates ideas and feelings with effectiveness.	Confidently and effectively communicates ideas and feelings.
• uses movement and drama language to create and analyze movement piece	Uses movement language and terms in creating and analyzing with limited effectiveness.	Uses movement language and terms in creating and analyzing with some effectiveness.	Uses movement language and terms in creating and analyzing with considerable effectiveness.	Uses movement language and terms in creating and analyzing with high degree of effectiveness
Application • applies skills, (concentration, control)	Moves with limited concentration and control.	Moves with some concentration and control.	Moves considerable concentration and control.	Concentrates and controls movement throughout rehearsal and performance.
• makes connections within and between contexts (e.g., dreams of ancestors and our dreams today)	Makes connections between contexts (past and present) with limited understanding and effectiveness.	Makes connections between contexts (past and present) with some understanding and effectiveness.	Makes connections between contexts (past and present) with considerable understanding and effectiveness.	Makes connections between contexts (past and present) with a high degree of understanding and effectiveness.

Pembroke Publishers ©2010 *Drama Schemes, Themes & Dreams* by Larry Swartz and Debbie Nyman ISBN 978-1-55138-253-1

Home

Being a refugee means many things to me. The war broke many families apart. The family of the place where you are born is the closest thing that you have in your life. When you leave your country, you still think about the country in your head, and you never forget. You are always back there in your heart.

—Taef Tozi, refugee from Iraq, age 13 years old, from *Making it Home*

Drama Theme: The Refugee Experience

This unit is not only about looking outside our windows, but also about opening our doors. The theme explores the thoughts and feelings of people who have lost their homes and can never return to them again.

How can we ever reconcile losing our homes? How can those who are forced to leave their countries move forward step-by-step to find shelter and belonging, to strengthen their identity and culture, and to maintain pride and independence? By considering the plight of fictional and real people, it is the intention of this theme to have students wrestle with how we, as a society, can take responsibility to help those citizens of the world who are refugees. As the work progresses, students can come to appreciate the place they call home.

The drama work is intended to illuminate students' own experiences and contemplation of where they live and how they live.

> Only one letter marks the difference between the words "home" and "hope."
> —Larry Swartz

LEARNING OPPORTUNITIES

- To develop an understanding of humanitarian issues through a variety of perspectives/roles
- To help students use and communicate ideas through drama work (e.g., role-playing, storytelling, meetings) and a variety of other art forms (e.g., visual arts, film, documentary, writing)
- To help students make text-to-world and fictional-to-real-world connections
- To explore different forms of dramatic presentations and analysis as both audience and performer
- To challenge students' personal views and feelings about refugees and asylum seekers
- To develop students' knowledge and understanding of the reasons why refugees have been forced to leave their countries of origin

- To develop students' understanding that, above all, refugees are individuals, just like themselves.

Launching the Drama: Games that Build Cooperation

1. DESIGNING A HOUSE

In this activity, students work spontaneously in a variety of group situations. They work with different people in each situation and should be encouraged to work with the same class member only once.

- The students' task is to decorate a house, using their bodies to represent various parts of a house.
- On a signal, students work

  - Alone to create a *plant*
  - In pairs to create a *lamp*
  - In groups of three to make an *MP3 player (add sounds)*
  - In groups of four to make a *painting for over a couch*
  - In groups of five to create a *backyard*
  - In groups of six to create a *bedroom*
  - Whole-class to create a *kitchen*

- Once students have created each item, the game is repeated.
- Randomly call out different items and students re-create the image in the space where they first prepared it, with the people they worked with.

2. PICTIONARY

- The class is divided into groups of four or five. Each group is given a large sheet of paper and a few markers of any color. The members of the group are numbered off—1, 2, 3, 4.
- Call the 1 members together and tell them a word that they are going to draw: e.g., basement, cottage, garden, etc. Each word could be written on a card. For purposes of this theme, each of the words chosen can relate to the topic of home:

  Home words: *bungalow, castle, cave, attic, condominium, address*
  Titles: *Little House on the Prairie, Home Alone, The Three Little Pigs, Home of the Brave*
  Phrases: *home free, home cooking, home run, homework*

- The 1 members rush back to their groups and, on a signal, begin to communicate the word by drawing quickly on the paper.
- The first group to guess the word correctly wins. Scores can be kept.
- The game is repeated until each member has had a chance to draw.

Extension

Repeat the game as a relay. The 1 members are the first to draw pictures. As soon as a group guesses the word, the 2 member goes to the teacher to get a new word for the group to guess; as soon as the group has guessed this word, member 3 receives a word to play; and so on. The first team to finish wins.

3. BACK HOME

- Students are arranged into groups of ten to fifteen players. They sit on chairs arranged in a circle. It is important that each chair touches the one beside it.
- One player volunteers to stand up and be It. It's chair is removed.
- Give a signal for everyone to quickly move to the right. It looks for an opportunity to get back into a chair.
- Any student can choose to stay in his or her chair instead of moving; he or she knocks on the chair beside him/her shouting out, "Back home." The circle then moves in the opposite direction.

4. HOME FREE!

- Spread newspapers around the room. Each newspaper represents a home base.
- Students start walking around the room without touching the papers.
- When you call out, "Home," the students rush to a paper to get home safely.
- Encourage students to help one another so that all players are "rescued." As the game progresses, remove papers to make it more challenging for students to secure a place home.

Extension

Musical accompaniment can be used for this activity. Students move to the music and wander about the room. Teacher stops the music and students are challenged to find a home space by landing on the paper.

Framing the Theme: Focus on Communication

A DEFINITION OF HOME

Students work in groups to write a dictionary definition of the word "home" using the following context:

A new dictionary is about to be published, but "home" has yet to be defined. Students, as dictionary editors, have been called upon for their input. They are given file cards to write their definitions of "home." Then they work with a partner to compare definitions.

These options could also be provided:

- Partners can work together to create a single definition.
- To make the activity more challenging, students can work in small groups to collaborate on a definition. The definition has to be exactly 25 words long.
- Tell the students that the new dictionary will be strictly visual, so that all definitions must be represented without words. Students create an image or design to represent "home."

WORD WEB

Students work in groups to brainstorm words that connect to the topic of homes. Some branching topics can include

- Kinds of homes
- Rooms in the house
- Locations of homes
- Titles (songs, movies, books)
- "Home" in other languages

PROVERBS

Offer the students the following proverbs, each connected to the topic of home.

- People who live in glass houses shouldn't throw stones.
- Home is where the heart is.
- There's no place like home.
- Home, Sweet Home.
- You can't go home again.
- A house is not a home.

This activity can be done in pairs with each student choosing a proverb to discuss. Alternatively, each proverb can be assigned to a group of students to discuss. Using the jigsaw technique, students can be reorganized into groups with each person being an "expert" on one of the proverbs. Discussion can include

- What does this proverb invite them to think about?
- Do they agree with the message of this proverb?
- What stories from fiction or real life are they familiar with that provide an example of this proverb?

BIRD HOUSE ARCHITECTS

Note: Each of the envelopes should contain items of a different quantity and/or quality. For example, some envelopes might have only a few materials, and perhaps exclude scissors and tape. Another envelope might have fancy paper, feathers, pipe cleaners, glitter, several pairs of scissors, etc.

Students are arranged into groups of four or five. Each group is given an envelope or box that contains a variety of materials to create a home (e.g., markers, scissors, toothpicks, paper, feathers, etc.). Tell students that they have been hired as architects to design a new bird house to be used in their community. The bird houses will be judged on originality, use of materials, and sturdiness. Each group member can contribute to the creation of the bird house.

Following the activity, students can examine each other's creations to determine how successfully each met the criteria for designing the bird house. The students should have an opportunity to discuss how they felt about their creation and to consider how this activity informs them about equity issues.

Extension

As a further challenge, students can be told that they are not allowed to speak as they work together to build their bird house. This instruction encourages non-verbal communication, negotiation, and problem-solving.

Students are invited to consider one of the windows that they look out of from their home (bedroom, kitchen, living room). Challenge students to draw a picture to show what they see when they look out the window on any given day. Encourage the students to consider small details as well as the larger picture. Once they are done, students can share their drawings with each other.

Questioning Our Questioning

by Steve Lieberman, former teacher, Peel District Board of Education

Recently, I modeled a drama lesson within a Grade 8 classroom, based on enhancing students' questioning skills and looking at a problem from different viewpoints. The picture book, *The Arrival* by Shaun Tan, offers many opportunities for exploring the emigrant and immigrant perspectives.

I organized the class into pairs and invited one of the two to become a newspaper reporter who had been assigned the task of interviewing immigrants to a new land. They were to gather information about those "who arrived," and be prepared to present their findings to the editors. The other partner was involved in the event, and was told to provide information only when asked (in other words, they were asked to not volunteer information). The class was then given time to begin their interviews and gather the information needed for the reporter to retell the story. It was interesting to hear the various interviews, as I went from group to group, listening but not contributing. After a few minutes, I stopped the class and asked each reporter to stand. When selected, each reporter began a recount of the events that he/she just heard about through their interviewing. The recounts were insightful and many reporters were quite descriptive. Several reporters explained that they experienced some frustration in getting only one-word answers and not the details. I myself had a question: How can I help the students to ask questions to get better answers?

I next asked the class to try to recall some of the questions that they had asked or heard during the interview. I recorded the beginnings of these questions on chart paper, and it was interesting to find that the majority of the questions asked were of the factual type. In essence, they could be answered in one word or even with a short phrase. I then introduced the students to a Q Chart and we discussed the different types of questions that could be asked.

With the Q Chart left on display for the students, I asked the reporter in each group to move to a different partner and switch roles. The new reporter was asked to sit so they could look at their partner and the Q Chart at the same time. It was interesting to once again listen to the different interviews. This time, the reporters made an effort to vary the types of questions that they were asking, and this led to a greater wealth of information being passed along. After a few minutes, the interviewers were asked to recall and retell the interview to the rest of the class. It was interesting to find that the students themselves noticed a difference in the stories that were gathered and retold. To enrich stories, in role and out of role, and to get better answers, it is essential—as Norah Morgan and Juliana Saxton inform us so well in their excellent resource—that we keep *Asking Better Questions*.

Q Chart

	Who	What	Where	When	Why	How
is						
did						
can						
might						
would						
will						

A Drama Structure Using Fictional Documents

MOVING ON: PERSONAL NARRATIVE

In groups, students told stories about when they moved. Students shared reasons why their families chose to move or were forced to move. Some students shared stories about moving to new neighborhoods, others shared stories about immigrating.

IMAGES OF HOME: CREATING SCULPTURES

Students were arranged into groups of four or five, numbered 1 to 4 or 5. To begin, the teacher invited students to think about the word "home" and what it means to them personally: How might each person in the group represent "homeness" into an image? Number 1 members began by molding an image using each member of the group. This activity was done in silence, and the number 1 would sculpt the image as if he/she were the sculptor creating the image. When complete, number 1 members stepped inside the image, becoming part of the scene. Music was used as background to this activity, to help create a mood as well as to encourage control and focus as they sculpted.

Each number 2 then stepped out and reshaped the image according to his/her interpretation. When complete, number 2 stepped inside the image, becoming part of the scene. The activity continued until each person had a chance to be sculptor.

Some students chose to represent a literal/concrete depiction, while others considered abstract.

As a final activity, the whole class built a collaborative image of home. One person volunteered to stand in the centre of the room to re-create his or her image from the group. Students randomly came forward to build on to the image. Students connected in some way to others that preceded them, until each student had joined in.

Reflection

- How did you feel about the sculptor role? Being sculpture?
- What were each of the images that you became in this exercise?
- How did the images deepen your understanding of home?

WHO IS A REFUGEE?: DISCUSSION

In groups, students shared personal stories (or stories of someone they knew) describing the circumstances of their families coming to Canada. Did they choose to come? Were they forced to move to another country?

The teacher discussed with the students the difference between an immigrant and refugee.

An immigrant chooses to come to a country, a refugee is at the mercy of a country granting asylum.

The students were provided with the definition of *refugee*. They were asked: What information do they learn by reading the definition? What challenges might a refugee face?

We do not really see through our eyes or hear through our ears, but through our beliefs. To put our beliefs on hold is to cease to exist as ourselves for a moment—and that is not easy. It is painful as well, because it means turning yourself inside out, giving up your own sense of who you are, and being willing to see yourself in the unflattering light of another's angry gaze. It is not easy, but it is the only way to learn what it might feel like to be someone else and the only way to dialogue.

—Lisa Delpit, *Other People's Children: Cultural conflict in the classroom* (1995/2006: 47)

A refugee is someone who has been forced to flee his or her country because of persecution, war, or violence. A refugee has a well-founded fear of persecution for reasons of race, religion, nationality, political opinion or membership in a particular social group. Most likely, they cannot return home or are afraid to do so. War and ethnic, tribal and religious violence are leading causes of refugees fleeing their countries.

—The UN Refugee Agency www.unrefugees.org

—www.amnesty.ca

LEAVING HOME: STILL IMAGES

The students brainstormed five reasons why someone might have to leave their home. They selected one of the reasons and created an image to represent this reason. To share the images, they returned to the last "Images of Home" tableau (see page 117) and, in slow motion, moved into the "Reason for Leaving" tableau. They shared the images seamlessly in a circle and then identified and discussed the reasons why someone might have to leave their homes. Students depicted violence, natural disasters such as hurricanes, and eviction or poverty in their tableaux. Students also discussed the implications of having to leave your home. Students talked about the possibility of being separated from family, not being able to rebuild in the same place, etc.

IN YOUR POCKET: TEACHER VOICE-OVER

Students froze in their depiction of leaving and, in a voice-over, the teacher asked them to imagine something that they would put into their pockets on the way out the door, thinking that they might never return again—something they might need to remember home.

> Imagine you and your family have been forced to leave home. You only have a short bit of time to prepare for your departure. Consider one item that you would take with you that would fit into your pocket.

ARRIVAL: MEETING

A meeting was established to set the context for the drama exploration. The teacher, in role as a Government Bureaucrat, entered. The students were sitting in chairs in a circle to prepare for a high-status role. Working in this way, students knew that their roles would become apparent and evolve as they listened and responded to information from the teacher in role.

> Thank you for coming here today. You have been contacted because of your expertise and interest in this matter. We have a crisis. There is at least one plane of refugees arriving later today. We need to be ready for them when they arrive. I am heading up this mission but I have to tell you that I am counting on you to advise me and prepare me to handle this situation.
>
> I know you will have questions and I will try to answer as best I can at this time. (*Teacher should be encouraging the questions, not necessarily giving the answers.*) We don't have time for formal introductions, so before I take your questions, I want to give you an opportunity to introduce yourself and say what you are most concerned with in terms of these young refugees.

WELCOME TO OUR COUNTRY: GROUP PLANNING

The students were arranged in groups of four or five, with the task of devising and rehearsing a plan of action to show us what it would look like when they would greet the young refugees. Students prepared presentations that depicted what would take place upon the arrival. Some chose to include a refugee in their scene; i.e., offering clothing, presenting food, translating instructions, etc. Others prepared signs, chants, cheers, and songs to greet them.

Following the presentations, they shared their thinking behind the choices by considering the following questions:

- What do you think would be urgent for the refugee to know? Learn?
- How might you want to be greeted if you moved to a new country?
- How do you think the young refugees would respond to these demonstrations?
- What did you hope to achieve by preparing in this way?

WILL YOU TAKE A REFUGEE INTO YOUR HOME? PAIRED IMPROVISATION

Through role taking, students may discover a more complex sense of other, they may also discover more complex of selfs or multiple subjectivities that now includes, as a result of their role taking, a confident self, a powerful self, a risk-taking self, a compassionate self.

—Jonothan Neelands, "The Space in Our Hearts," speech given in Toronto, 2001

Working in partners A and B, A played the role of a refugee worker asking B, in the role of the head of a household, if they would open up their homes to a refugee, in particular a 14-year-old boy, for an unknown period of time. The students role-played for a few minutes, and then were questioned in the whole group by the teacher.

Forming two circles with pairs sitting together, one behind the other, A partners sat in the inside circle and were questioned by the teacher reflecting on the role play:

- Was your partner willing to take in a refugee? Why or why not?
- What questions did they have? What concerns did they share?
- Was there anything they need or want from us to make this work?

The teacher then questioned the B partners:

- Were you willing to take a refugee into your home?
- What are you worried about?
- How do you think your family will respond?
- What can we do to support you?

REFUGEE CASE STUDY: WHOLE-CLASS IMPROVISATION

Teacher entered in role of an immigration worker, speaking to the students in the role of refugee case workers/social workers. The teacher addressed the students:

We are meeting today to work out the details of the placement of Tek, a newly arrived boy. We want to place him in a family temporarily until we can make permanent arrangements for him. He has spent some time in a refugee camp. We have his file here and hope that, after you spend some time with it, you will be able to help him further. This is all we know about him right now. We must closely examine the information to make the best choices for him. He has traveled a long way alone. Please study the file and together we will find accommodation for him.

The teacher distributed the file (see Case Study on page 121). Students worked in small groups to examine it.

WHERE WILL TEK LIVE?: REPORTING IN ROLE

Students were given time to examine the Tek document and made two lists: What we know for sure/What we would like to know.

They shared their lists and created one together. The students then returned to their groups and made four recommendations for how to place Tek with a family. Some students recommended that there be other children, that the family speak his language; others felt he should learn the new language, that he have privacy and be close to school. The students shared their recommendations in an oral report to the teacher in role as the refugee worker.

TEK'S NEW HOME: SMALL-GROUP IMPROVISATION

The teacher moved the drama forward with the following narration:

> Tek was placed in a home with other children as recommended and he was enrolled in the local school. He faced many challenges in the first few days and weeks.

The students considered the events in what might be an average day for Tek early in his stay with his new family. Students decided on the following scenes:

- Breakfast, getting ready for school
- School cafeteria at lunch
- A moment in the classroom
- After-school activities
- Dinnertime
- Saying goodnight

Students worked in small groups and selected a moment or event that they were interested in exploring through developing a short scene, beginning with a tableau. The scene would show Tek and his new family or schoolmates in this particular moment. The scene did not have to have a definite ending. If the student spoke another language, they could play the role of Tek and speak a language other than English; or Tek could be silent in the scenes and not speak. While the students were preparing, the teacher visited each group and challenged them to be authentic and truthful: if the students playing Tek did choose to speak another language, they were encouraged to work hard to stay in role while they worked.

WITNESSING TEK'S LIFE: PRESENTING DRAMA WORK

Students rehearsed for a few minutes and then prepared to share the scenes. The scenes were arranged in the room in chronological order, and the students were told that, while they were audience and watching the scenes, they would also be in role as the refugee social workers watching to learn about Tek in his new home and to assess how well he was adjusting. To further understand, they would at times be given the opportunity to question the actors in the scenes. The teacher

Case Study

Refugee Status

First Name: Tek, short for Tekle
Last Name: Adishu
Age: 14 years
Birthday: unknown

LEVEL OF PROFICIENCY IN ENGLISH: Tek knows a few words in English. He has had some formal schooling in his native language before arriving at the refugee camp.

PHYSICAL DESCRIPTION: Tek is 5' 7". He is tall for his age and very thin. He is in good health. He has a quiet voice and gentle manner.

BRIEF DESCRIPTION OF CASE: Tek was away from home working in the fields when his village was attacked. He heard the sounds of gunfire and airplanes. He hid in the forest until it was over. When he returned to his village, his family was gone.

INTERESTS: Tek enjoys football (soccer) and singing. He loves to draw. He uses vivid colors in his drawings. Hs favorite color is green. He has said that he would like to be a teacher when he grows up.

SPECIAL CIRCUMSTANCES: Tek lived with his aunt and uncle briefly after he lost his family, but after a few months they could not afford to keep him with them. He has been in a refugee camp for the last six months. He has not heard from his family—mother, father, brother. He is hopeful but he often sits alone and seems sad. He carries a small piece of green cloth in his pocket with him at all times.

Pembroke Publishers ©2010 *Drama Schemes, Themes & Dreams* by Larry Swartz and Debbie Nyman ISBN 978-1-55138-253-1

could enter the scene at any time in the role of the social worker to meet with and to also question the new people in Tek's life.

The teacher informed students that she might revisit a scene, and they could then continue where they left off or replay it. For this purpose, they needed to be in role as social workers while watching the scenes, but always ready to return to their scenes with a cue from the teacher. As the students shared the scenes, the teacher moved into the scenes briefly and questioned the students in role.

At different points, when it seemed there was a need for clarification or to deepen the work, the teacher invited the audience in role to also ask questions. The teacher acted as conductor and revisited some scenes, invited the social workers into some scenes, and continued until she felt the students had created a shared picture of Tek's new life. The students then regrouped as social workers and discussed Tek's adjustment: Was he adjusting to his new life? What support could be offered to make the adjustment easier? What did they see for him in the future?

CULMINATING ACTIVITY: THROUGH TEK'S EYES

As a culminating moment, students returned to the tableau that opened the scene. Without any discussion, the student in role of Tek was asked what he might want to change in the picture, and then he reshaped, molded the people in the image to show the change. Students remained frozen in their tableaux and glanced around the room to see the new images.

Reflection

Following the scene exploration, students discussed the process (the theatrical conventions) and the context (Tek's adjustment and circumstances). Students responded to the following questions:

- Which scenes drew you in as an audience?
- How did questioning the actors deepen your understanding of the situation?
- What challenges did you face as an actor working this way? How did you meet these challenges?
- What did you further learn about Tek? How do you think he is adjusting?
- How can the refugee workers support Tek and the family? What actions might they take to improve the situation?

In the following quotation, Dorothy Heathcote explains how the work is deepened by giving the students a role as they watch each other's work. In this way, they are given "permission to stare," making the work more meaningful.

> I spend a lot of time preventing classes feeling stared at. ...The obvious way of avoiding this is to give them something so attractive in the room that they feel they are staring at it. Role is one of the most efficient "others." What I am discussing here is that "the other" be the gateway to all the full depth of exploration which will follow as the class get involved with the issues.
> —Dorothy Heathcote from *Collected writings on education and drama* edited by Liz Johnson and Cecily O'Neill (1984)

Assessment: Focus on Problem-solving Skills

How successfully does the student demonstrate an ability to

- communicate?
- question?
- argue?
- persuade?
- negotiate?
- brainstorm?
- hypothesize?
- take risks?
- collaborate?
- reflect?

Following the sharing of the scenes, students were asked to write in role as either Tek or a member of his new family. The drama was moved ahead six months and the students wrote a journal entry to mark the six-month anniversary, either in the role of Tek or as a member of the new family. Students shared their writing, sitting in two circles, with the students who had written in the role of Tek in the inside circle and students who had written in the role of a member of his new family in the outside circle. The teacher randomly chose students by tapping them on the shoulder to read aloud an excerpt from their writing.

Considering the Work of Augusto Boal
by Julia Balaisis, drama educator, OISE/UT

Theatre is born when the human being discovers that it can observe itself... observing itself the human being perceives what it is, discovers what it is not and imagines what it could become.
—from Augusto Boal, *The Rainbow of Desire*

I have found the work of Augusto Boal, and his Theatre of the Oppressed, to be particularly compelling for adolescents and teens. Students, at the threshold of adulthood, are at work to individuate—separate and distinguish themselves from parental, familial, and societal culture—and therefore can easily identify with the themes of oppression. Coming into conflict—or, at least, questioning authority figures, societal norms, and standards and figuring out one's place in the world—opens students up to the rich exploratory conventions that Boal offers.

ImageTheatre, *Forum Theatre*, and *Invisible Theatre*, along with *Rainbow of Desire* and *Cops in the Head*, afford a full gamut of techniques to address the myriad concerns and interests that confront our students. Everything, from the most personal to the collective, from debacles with authority to global distress, have a Boalian strategy that "fits" best for such examination through dramatic play.

In my experience, students, with their age-appropriate insurgency, incline not only to the philosophical stance of Boal (whereby he overturns traditional Aristotelian notions of theatre with an audience sitting passively to experience catharsis and proper socialization), but also to his active and expressive techniques that encourage personal content, rich verbal expressions, and bodily freedom. The lovely Boalism of changing spectators into *spect-actors* captures the essence of his revolutionary notions about theatre.

In this theatre for social and personal change, students are empowered with autonomy right from the outset where they choose *their* issues of the day that will become the content for the drama. These may include everything from personal relational dilemmas; to conflicts with parents, teachers, and other authority figures; to larger society and global issues.

I usually start Boal work by having students work imagistically with the notions of oppressor and oppressed. We explore status as a group and get the juices further flowing by filling in the spaces, pair work, and sculpting statues of oppressor and oppressed images. Nice complements to this work are found in the status work of Keith Johnstone (*Impro: Improvisation and Theatre* by Keith Johnstone).

After students get their bodies working in these polar realities, the stories can (and will) start to flow. Again, I work with image theatre before moving on to words. A simple group exercise may be to create a wordless scene of oppressor and oppressed, with little planning time at all. I trust that students organically know where to go with this. And they never disappoint, since their lives are filled with moment-to-moment status plays.

After we have worked sufficiently with these energies, we can begin to conceptualize student stories and add content, always allowing students sufficient anonymity to maintain the safety that role affords them. Content varies: bully situations, problems with rules and procedures, decisions around relationships, etc. I, as teacher, then pair the stories up with the most appropriate Boalian strategy for exploration. For example, internal conflict calls for Cops in the Head; indecision or difficult choices call for Rainbow of Desire; dilemmas that are more social (and where we can delineate a protagonist and antagonist, either personal or collective) can be put out to Forum Theatre.

A positive example of how Forum Theatre has done its healing and transformative work is illustrated by a student who, watching his fellow spect-actors fill his shoes again and again (as students call "stop" and take turns moving into the scene as protagonist), came to work out a significant conflictual dilemma with his parents (over control and boundary issues) in a way that maintained his own integrity, and communicated his needs with healthy assertion while not threatening the loving bond and relationship that still anchored him.

An added benefit of Forum Theatre is that all individual stories meld into everyone else's personal story so all have the opportunity to gain from the experience. Again and again, in the process of a forum, we have witnessed "aha!" moments when the drama has achieved its purpose (of finding the best way) and is, essentially, complete.

As a teacher, over the years I have learned to be guided by the following principles in doing Boal work:

1. Choose to work only with topics or stories that have personal relevance and an emotional charge. (Topics that were too emotionally distant, albeit important, like a fateful drama on capital punishment, went nowhere.)
2. Ensure that there is sufficient protection in role for students who disclose many personal details. Help them be safe: change names and details when necessary.
3. Action speaks louder, and is in many cases more profound, than words. If in doubt, choose to do any Boal convention through movement and watch how remarkably it communicates.
4. Be reminded that we are not therapists and should not think that we can do therapy with a student. Boal called his work "therapeutic," but not therapy.
5. Invisible theatre (for those who venture there) is exciting, but not for the faint of heart.

Some titles by Augusto Boal

Games for Actors and Non-actors, 2nd edition (2002)
Hamlet and the Baker's Son: My life in theatre and politics (2001)
The Rainbow of Desire: The Boal method of theatre and therapy (1995)
Theatre of the Oppressed (1997)

Definition of Terms

Cops in the Head: A dynamic strategy for examining our limiting constraints (imported from various voices in our lives), whereby spectators embody them using image, movement, and action while fighting with the protagonist.
Forum Theatre: The spectators intervene directly in the dramatic action, posed as a dilemma with a protagonist and antagonist, and act with the help of a "joker" who moderates the process.
Image Theatre: The spectators intervene directly, "speaking" through images made with the actors' bodies.
Invisible Theatre: The presentation of a scene in an environment other than the theatre, before people who are not spectators. The people who witness the scene are there by chance, without the slightest idea that it is a "spectacle."
Rainbow of Desire: A dynamic strategy for examining possibilities, whereby spectators embody and represent various choices using image, movement, and action while interacting with the protagonist.

Extending the Drama

RESEARCH THE REFUGEE STORY

Invite the students to use the Internet to learn more about refugees from Africa and other parts of the world. Have them identify real agencies that place refugees.

LAST FLIGHT TO HAITI

See newspaper article on page 126. 1. Students are provided copies of a newspaper article. Students are given a file card to write:

  • one sentence from the article that interested them about the refugees

- a question that they would ask the reporter about her report
- a new headline that they think might encapsulates this article

Students exchange file cards and share their responses.

2. Students are arranged in four different groups. Each group is provided with a different context for presenting the themes and story in the article:

GROUP ONE: An *interview* between reporters and one or two experts involved with the evacuation

GROUP TWO: A *podcast* to depict the evacuation of the children. Quotations from the experts could be included.

GROUP THREE: An improvised *scene* that dramatizes the story (e.g., departing the country, on the plane, upon arrival).

GROUP FOUR: Tell the story in a series of *tableaux*. These still images could represent the photographs that would appear in a magazine article about the story.

Following the presentations ask the students:
- What is the key idea about the topic that is communicated in each presentation?
- What else could the politicians and concerned citizens do to help the children and adults of this country?
- What actions can we take to assist refugees around the world?

Opportunities for researching support groups and assistance are available on the Internet. See websites on page 172.

CREATING A DOCUMENTARY

Tell the students to imagine that they have been hired as filmmakers to create a documentary about refugees. Working in small groups, students plan what should be included in the documentary. Students consider which people they will they include (i.e., Whose voices will tell the story?), the events and interviews that will be featured, the locations that will be shared. As filmmakers, students need to consider the order of scenes, a title for their project, the variety of images that will be included, etc. Once prepared, documentary filmmakers can pitch their ideas to a producer.

The drama classroom should not be made post-human; on the contrary, technology can be used in drama to put the human experience at the centre of learning.
—from *Real Players? Drama, technology and education* by John Carroll, Michael Anderson and David Cameron

Extension

Students can rehearse and present an opening scene for their documentary. If students have access to the technology, they can prepare a brief video that they might use to pitch their ideas to potential producers.

ADVICE TO NEW REFUGEES

Students work in small groups to prepare a list of recommendations for assisting refugees to become familiar and comfortable in their new home. Once completed, two groups work together to share lists. Challenge the students to prioritize the five most significant items to be considered.

A MEMORY OF HOME: STORYTELLING

Invite the students to remember, in the Tek case study (see Case Study on page 121), the reference to the piece of cloth that he carries with him in his pocket. Ask

January 29, 2010

Operation Stork winds down

By Jane Taber

Globe and Mail Update

The Air Canada Airbus A330 was just beginning its descent into Port-au-Prince last Saturday when the message came through the cockpit's data system from the airline's operations centre: "Attn: AC2150: Confirmed 24 children for your return. Take care of them."

There were high fives all around.

Captain Chris Pulley, his colleagues, Captains Jean Castonguay and Eddy Doyle, and Air Canada's chief operating officer Duncan Dee, who was travelling with them, had been waiting for this news. They were thrilled because they were bringing to Canada the very first group of Haitian orphans to some very anxious parents.

> How immigration officials, airline staff and everyone except Big Oil pitched in to evacuate dozens of orphans

This Saturday, Mr. Dee and other Air Canada officials are flying back to Haiti; it is expected they will bring back another 57 orphans. A group of 52 orphans arrived in Ottawa Wednesday.

It is likely, however, this will be the last flight of orphans.

"The numbers should taper off after that because those are the bulk of the children for whom we have received approval from the provincial adoption agencies," Immigration Minister Jason Kenney told The Globe and Mail.

Immigration officials had initially identified a list of 154 children, whose cases were far enough along that they could be expedited to Canada. Most of them, including those on this weekend's flight, have been brought to Canada.

The Haitian government is now discouraging the adoption of orphans not in the process prior to the earthquake. There are concerns about child trafficking.

And so what Immigration Canada has dubbed "Operation Stork," is winding down.

It began several days after the Jan. 12 earthquake. After receiving calls from MPs with anxious constituents in the process of adopting Haitian orphans and hearing their stories in the press, it became clear that it was crucial these children were brought out.

It wasn't easy.

One big problem was finding someone in the Haitian government to deal with. Indeed, things were so chaotic, Mr. Kenney was hearing reports that even bureaucrats in the Haitian agriculture department were signing off on allowing children to leave.

Finally, that practice was shut down and emergency powers were centralized with Haitian Prime Minister Jean-Max Bellerive.

As it happened, Canada's ambassador in Haiti, Gilles Rivard, was meeting with the Prime Minister about a week after the quake. The ambassador was given the list of 154. He presented it to the Prime Minister, who signed off on it. Canadian officials in Haiti scouted around to the orphanages, locating the children.

And then last Friday, Mr. Kenney called Mr. Dee, who is a friend. Between 60 and 80 orphans were ready to come out, he said. Could Air Canada help?

Mr. Dee, whose company has done this before, evacuating children from New Orleans after Hurricane Katrina, jumped into action.

Air Canada's caregiver list was activated, as was their medical team, including a doctor who specializes in the effects of cabin air pressure on diseases while in flight. There were concerns about collapsed lungs among the children. An Air Canada customer service agent in Montreal, Jacqueline Dupont, who is known for her baking, baked all day, providing dozens of small cakes and muffins for the orphans.

Everyone volunteered their time; several of the airline's suppliers donated their services, including supplying food on board, waiving of airport landing charges and air navigation fees. Not the oil companies, however. Air Canada asked the fuel suppliers to donate and were refused.

As the flight left Canada last Saturday, carrying about 35 tonnes of humanitarian aid, the crew still had no idea how many orphans would be returning. Indeed, one orphanage director with 20 children destined for Canada refused at the last minute to allow her charges to leave. They were on Wednesday's flight.

Early last Sunday morning as the orphans boarded the plane in Haiti for Canada, the flight's service director Bob Nolan grabbed the intercom: "We thank God for your presence with us this evening," he said. "You are about to embark on a very exciting adventure." As they landed in Ottawa, Mr. Nolan said: "Ladies and gentlemen, boys and girls, welcome to Canada, welcome home."

Pembroke Publishers ©2010 *Drama Schemes, Themes & Dreams* by Larry Swartz and Debbie Nyman ISBN 978-1-55138-253-1

the students to consider the importance of this object: imagining who might have given it to him; where and when he received it; and why he chooses to carry it with him. Invite students to create the story of the green cloth. Students can write the story or retell it to a partner.

IN YOUR POCKET: REVISITED

Invite the students to revisit the earlier activity (page 118) and remember the object they placed in their pockets as they fled their homes. Ask the students to consider the significance of this object for them and why they chose it. Invite the students to sit in a circle and share their imaginary or real objects with each other. Begin the activity with the line, "As I left my home for maybe the last time, I tucked _____ into my pocket."

ELEVATOR SPEECH

An Elevator Message or Speech is an opportunity for people to comment, give opinions, or persuade someone to consider a point of view. In an elevator you are challenged to have a conversation in a brief period of time before someone arrives at their floor destination. Students can prepare an elevator speech to convince someone about the importance of admitting refugees into the community.

Script Variation: Dialogue

"David French has a way of making plays that belong to us. They belong to us as artists, they belong to us as Canadians, they belong to us as parents, and they belong to us as children."
— Albert Schultz, Artistic Director, Soulpepper Theatre Company

Leaving Home by David French is a classic Canadian play that tells the story of the Mercers, a Newfoundland family that has lost its way after emigrating. Jacob the father, a laborer, is fiercely committed to creating and sustaining a home for his family. There is growing tension between the generations and, in the play, Jacob's fears come to pass when both sons decide to move out. Bill and Ben are anxious to leave home, while their parents cannot imagine a home without the two boys. The sequel, *Of the Fields, Lately,* finds son Ben returning home to find his mother trying to care for his father after a heart attack. Rounding out the trilogy is the prequel, *Salt-Water Moon,* focusing on Mary, a fierce teenager with "steel in her heart."

Other strategies for exploring script can be found in Chapter 8: Dreams Aloud.

By exploring the excerpt on page 130, students are given opportunities to develop their understanding of "homeness" by considering the different perspectives of those who live together. Though written several decades ago, the trilogy is continually revised for performance. The themes in the Mercer Family Trilogy continue to be relevant to adolescents today. For every person, the word "home" has a different setting, a different story, and a different feeling, ranging from comfort to tension.

Strategy Scheme: Working with Dialogue Script

The script on page 130 is an example of a dialogue involving two characters. Students can explore different ways to rehearse and present a script with a partner. At any time during this process, students can switch parts to explore each of the characters.

1. Partners decide who is going to read the part of Mother/Son to read through the script.
2. Partners reread the script, reversing roles.
3. Students take turns exploring each of the roles. This time, assign the following attitudes to read the script each time:

   Mary is calm/Ben is nervous

   Mary is nervous/Ben is calm

   Mary is angry/Ben is nervous

   Mary is angry/Ben is angry

   Both are calm

4. Partners decide which role they are each more comfortable with. Partners also decide which attitude they think would be most authentic. Partners rehearse the scene
5. Two pairs match up. The Mothers from each scene switch so that each Ben has a new actor to work with. Students rehearse the scene. How did working with a new partner change the work?
6. Students return to their original pairs to direct the scene as if it were to be performed on stage. This activity can be done with partners making decisions on how to direct the scene. Alternatively, one pair of students can direct another pair. To rehearse the scene, students can consider the following.
   - Will the actors stand or sit?
   - What activity might one/both of the actors be doing?
   - Will there be a pause in between each line of dialogue?
   - What gestures (if any) will the actors use as they deliver their lines?
   - Will the actors have eye contact throughout the scene?
7. Once students are familiar with the script, they can work "off book" to rehearse the scene. Students can be encouraged to improvise lines, if needed.
8. Invite students to improvise the scene and continue the dialogue.
9. Partners can continue this scene by writing a dialogue script featuring the character of Ben and his mother.
10. Partners can exchange new scripts and practice reading scenes out loud.

In the excerpt from Act One of *Leaving Home* on page 130, the stage directions offer one suggestion of how the scene can be directed. Students can explore the script, paying attention to the stage directions. A further challenge is to omit stage directions and work with a partner to create stage directions.

PAIRED IMPROVISATION INTO SCRIPT

Students can choose (or be assigned) one of the following two-character scenes to improvise. To understand the different points of view, students should have an opportunity to role-play each of the characters in each scene.

- Ben and his father have a conversation.
- Mary and Father have a conversation about Ben leaving.
- Ben discusses his plans with his brother Billy.
- Billy and Kathy discuss the possibilities of Ben moving in.
- Billy has a conversation with Mary (or Father).

Extensions

a) Students create a new dialogue script based on their improvisation.
b) Students work in groups of four. Two partners take on the role of the director to rehearse the scene with the two actors.
c) After rehearsing the scenes, students share their improvisations to help an audience understand the decision that Ben has made to leave home. Consider: In what order will the scenes be presented?

Excerpt from *Leaving Home* by David French

BEN (urgently): Mom, there's something I want to tell you before Dad comes in.

MARY: Sure, my son. Go ahead. I'm listening. What's on your mind?

BEN: Well…

MARY (smiling): Come on. It can't be that bad.

BEN (slight pause): I want to move out, Mom

MARY (almost inaudibly): What?

BEN: I said I want to move out.

MARY (softly as she sets the cutlery): I heard you. (pause) What for?

BEN: I just think it's time. I'll be nineteen soon. (pause) I'm moving in with Billy and Kathy and help pay the rent. (pause) I won't be far away. I'll see you on weekends. (Mary nods) Mom?

MARY (absently): What?

BEN: Will you tell Dad? (slight pause) Mom? Did you hear me?

MARY: I heard you. He'll be upset, I can tell you. By rights you ought to tell him yourself.

BEN: If I do, we'll just get in a big fight and you know it. He'll take it better, coming from you.

Pembroke Publishers ©2010 *Drama Schemes, Themes & Dreams* by Larry Swartz and Debbie Nyman ISBN 978-1-55138-253-1

Assessment: Rubric for Evaluating Role Playing

Criteria	Limited	Sometimes	Often	Consistently
KNOWLEDGE and UNDERSTANDING	Demonstrates a limited understanding of the use of role to explore a range of perspectives.	Demonstrates some understanding of the use of role to explore a range of perspectives.	Demonstrates good understanding of the use of role to explore a range of perspectives.	Demonstrates a solid and confident understanding of the use of role to explore a range of perspectives.
COMMITMENT TO ROLE	Adopts the attitudes and point of view of role with limited ability.	Adopts the attitudes and point of view of role with some ability.	Adopts the attitudes and point of view of role with good ability.	Adopts the attitudes and point of view of role with solid and confident ability.
COMMUNICATION	Uses language and gestures in a limited way to communicate thoughts, feelings, and ideas.	Uses language and gestures in satisfactory ways to communicate thoughts, feelings, and ideas.	Uses language and gestures in appropriate ways to communicate thoughts, feelings, and ideas.	Uses language and gestures in deep ways to communicate thoughts, feelings, and ideas.
CRITICAL ANALYSIS and APPRECIATION	Reflects on personal learning in role to a limited degree.	Reflects on personal learning in role to some degree.	Reflects on personal learning in role to a significant degree.	Reflects on personal learning in role to a strong degree.

Pembroke Publishers ©2010 *Drama Schemes, Themes & Dreams* by Larry Swartz and Debbie Nyman ISBN 978-1-55138-253-1

CHAPTER 7

Mother, What Was War?

… every generation has to discover things for themselves, don't they? There's some things that can be understood through telling, but other things have to be experienced before they can be fully apprehended. War is one such thing.
—from *War Horse, Act 1, Scene 8* by Nick Stafford, based on the novel by Michael Morpurgo

Drama Theme: War

We cannot change history, but with love we can heal the future.

—Kim Phuc *The Girl in the Picture: the Story of the Story of Kim Phúc, the Photograph and the Vietnam War* by Denise Chong (1999)

War and Peace. Death and Loss. Heroes and Enemies. Arrivals and Departures. War is a time of opposites. It is a time of contradictions—a time of complexities. Through drama work, students can explore some of these complexities and experience the effects that war has on individuals and nations. By examining the roles of those who fight in war, as well as the lives of those who have been "left behind," students can consider some of the decisions, the dilemmas, and the stories of men and women caught in the web of battle. Every day, newspaper and magazine articles inform us of global events, perhaps involving our own countries, where thousands of troops have entered into combat. There has never been a time in history when the world has lived without war. War is the fodder for a wide range of cultural expression: literature, movies, television, music art, dance. This theme provides young people an opportunity to respond to a number of sources and to experience a range of artistic elements to help them grow in their understanding of the effects war has on the brave citizens who fight to defend.

LEARNING OPPORTUNITIES

- To consider the effects of war and empathize with those who participate in war and those who are left behind
- To share knowledge and understanding of war events throughout history
- To develop cooperation through activities focused on trust
- To develop students' empathy through role-playing
- To promote students' personal response to written text and photographs, and to build understanding by sharing their responses collaboratively
- To rehearse and present a public performance synthesizing drama techniques experienced during the theme; i.e., The Collective Creation
- To use writing in role both to build the drama experience and to reflect on the learning

Launching the Drama: Trust Games

1. TRUST WALK

- Working in pairs, students decide who is A and B.
- A agrees to close his/her eyes and B leads A through the room, stopping in various places for A to explore through sound and touch.
- A and B can hold hands or connect at the wrist or the shoulders; students uncomfortable with touch can be connected through a piece of cloth or rope.
- When partners return to the starting place, A shares with B his/her thoughts about where they were and how it felt to work with eyes closed.
- A then leads B through the room.

2. COMMANDERS

We teachers have enormous power to influence the future of the students in our care. We need to be mindful of that power and remain consistently conscious of what it means to teach fairly in an unfair world.

—Kathleen Gould Lundy, *Teaching Fairly in an Unfair World* (2008: 9)

- Working in pairs, students decide who is A and who is B.
- A is the controller and stands behind B.
- A places two fingers lightly on B's back and controls and guides B through the space with the following cues:
  - lightly tapping in the centre of the back indicates move straight ahead
  - tapping on the left shoulder indicates turn left
  - tapping on the right shoulder, turn right
  - to indicate *Stop*, the student stops tapping.
  The speed is regulated by slower or faster tapping.
- Students can play the game with eyes open at first; when they are comfortable, they can try it with eyes closed.

3. THE PROTECTORS

- Students walk around the room in a variety of ways—changing levels, speed, direction, etc.
- Ask students to continue walking and, in their minds and without telling anyone, to designate someone in the room, for the purposes of the game, to be someone they fear and keep their distance from.
- Students continue to walk about the room. Ask students to think of another person in the room to be their protector.
- Students continue to move through the room, not revealing their selected feared persons and protectors, but trying to keep the protectors close and the feared persons far from them.
- After a few minutes, call the group to freeze and have students disclose their feared persons and protectors.
- Students reflect on the game. Ask students to consider how successful they were at evading the ones they feared and keeping their protectors close. What were the challenges in the game? How might the game be connected to real-life situations?

Extension

As students move about the room, invite them to have two people that they are protecting. The challenge is to form a triangle, so that the three people are equidistant as they move about.

4. LOOK UP/LOOK DOWN (OR THE ENEMY)

- Students gather in a circle and lower their heads so that no one can see each other. Advise students that they are going to be on watch to seek out enemies.
- On a signal, students raise their heads and attempt to make eye contact with anyone in the circle.
- If two "enemies" have made eye contact, they eliminate themselves from the circle and the game is repeated until a final pair remain.

Extensions

a) A line of text is said out loud chorally by the group: e.g., "War, what is it good for?" When the last word of the text has been completed, this is a signal for all to raise their heads. The text is repeated each time as the game continues.
b) Sometimes, there is no eye contact made by any group members. In this case, each person calls out a word of their choice in a dramatic way. This is done spontaneously around the circle. Any player can choose to begin the shout-out and continue with each player on the right calling out. When complete, the group calls out "BRAVO!"

He who saves one life… it is as if he saves an entire universe. He who destroys a life, it is as if he does an entire universe.
— Talmud *Shendrin* 4:5

5. WINK

- The class is divided into two or three large groups, each forming a circle.
- Everyone is given a slip of paper. One slip in each group has an *X* marked on it. The person who receives the *X* is the "enemy." Alternatively, you can designate an enemy by tapping someone on the shoulder while everyone's eyes are closed.
- The designated enemy hunts down the prey by "winking" at another person in the group.
- The person winked at counts silently to ten before announcing, "I'm dead."
- If someone still not hunted in the group guesses who the enemy is, that person makes an accusation. If correct, the round is over, and the slips are drawn again. If wrong, the accuser is removed from the game. Can the enemy make all but one victim disappear?

Extensions

a) Repeat the game, joining two circles together. It is recommended that there be only one piece of paper marked *X* the first time the game is played in a large circle. The game, however, can be played with two enemies; an enemy cannot wink at another enemy.
b) Perform the game in one large group. Everyone draws a slip, but this time there are three or four enemies. The students wander around the room. The game proceeds in the same way except that, if a person gets hunted, he or she counts to ten and then "dies" in a very dramatic way.

Framing the Theme: Using Primary Resources

USING A PHOTOGRAPH

This photo, titled "Bring My Daddy Home," was taken by photographer Claud Detloff on October 1, 1940, in New Westminster, British Columbia. The next day it appeared in the *Province* newspaper, and five-year-old Warren "Whitey" Bernard became a celebrity.

- Students examine the photograph. In pairs, students share their first impressions of the image: e.g., what it reminds them of; how it makes them feel; the story they think is behind the picture.
- Working in pairs, students suggest titles for the photograph. Partners share their titles.
- Ask the students: Where would you want to be in this photograph? Encourage the students to give reasons for their choices.
- Students create a tableau to depict one person who might be in photograph. Each person creates the image and completes the sentence: "I am…"
- Students work in groups of four. Each group chooses one character who has been brought to life as a still image. Have students create a tableau "photo-

graph" that depicts this character some time before the picture was taken; e.g., an hour, a day, a week, a month prior. Each group could be assigned a specific time to focus on.

- Students conduct a gallery walk where each group shares their images. Each group has a number and, when called upon, they walk through the gallery, then return to their picture.
- Students discuss the images they presented. How did these images help tell the story behind the picture? What new information did we learn? What might the future story be?

Extensions

a) Students can write a message on the back of the photograph: either a caption or in role as one of the characters in the photograph. What advice, story, or memory will be included in the message?
b) Tell students that this photograph was featured on the front page of the newspaper/in a magazine article. Students can write a newspaper headline/a caption that might accompany this photograph. Some students may wish to write a short article that would accompany the photograph.

DESIGNING A WAR MEMORIAL

Students work in groups to design a war memorial. Instruct students that there will be a competition in the community and a decision will be made to determine which design will be chosen. Students are given time to consider the images that they wish to depict, the people or animals that might be included, and the arrangement of the sculpture.

Once completed, each artist group presents their model to the mayor of the community (i.e., teacher in role). Groups should be prepared describe their monument and to explain the reasons for their choices. The 'mayor' may question any of the group members by considering

- What has been included
- What has been excluded

Extensions

The Wave is an activity that encourages students to reflect through stillness and movement.

a) Students are arranged in a circle or walk in a line, shoulder to shoulder, usually in groups of eight to ten. On a signal from the teacher, the group begins moving slowly from one end of the room to another. As they move, individuals can choose to drop out of the line and freeze into a position representing war or peace. Group members who have not removed themselves continue to the end of the room, turn around, and return. In this way, individuals who have frozen get picked up by the wave, joining in and continuing with the group. The movement activity can be repeated.
b) Two groups on either end of the room can cross over to create the wave activity.

See "Exploring Art's Transformative Power" in *Story Drama* by David Booth (2005: 117) for a description of the lesson "The Monument by Gary Paulsen."

Music Suggestions

Cirque de Soleil (*Alegria, Quidam*)
Joshua Bell (*Voice of the Violin, Romance of the Violin*)
Erik Satie (*Gymnopédies*)
Enya (*The Very Best of Enya*)
Movie Adagios, Classical 96.3
Putamayo (*Acoustic Africa, World Playground*)
The Secret Garden (*Songs from a Secret Garden, Earthsongs*)
Yo-Yo Ma (*The Essential Yo-Yo Ma, Yo-Yo Plays Ennio Morricone*)

- Ask students to work in small groups and consider the answer to the following questions: What happens to the children living in a country under invasion? How would their lives change? Students share their responses with the class.
- Invite students to work in pairs. They are the heads of the household and family. They are responsible for the family. Ask the students to decide who they will be in this role: mother, father, oldest child, grandparent, etc. Inform them that it is late at night and their children are asleep. They have been told that their country is going to be at war, that troops are arriving. There will be soldiers in the streets. There will be bombs. There will be danger. In the role-play, they need to decide what they will do with the children, make a plan for the children.
- Following the role-play, invite the students to share their plans. The teacher can continue to challenge students with questions as they report to the class: e.g., Will they be safe at school? How will they get to school?
- Ask the students: If you were interviewing children living in a country at war, what would you want to ask them? Working in pairs, the students devise an interview. Instruct them to decide on the age and gender of the child being interviewed before they start. Ask students to generate a list of ten questions, and then highlight the question they feel is the most important for the world to know in answer to the question: How are children affected by war? Pairs can share their answers and create a list together.

THE CHILDREN OF WAR

Canadian author Deborah Ellis interviewed children of Canadian and American soldiers serving in Afghanistan and Iraq. The transcripts in the resource *Off to War: Voices of Soldiers' Children* reveal the authentic stories and describe the feelings of children and young adolescents whose mothers and fathers have chosen to serve. In *Children of War*, Ms. Ellis interviewed children who are currently refugees in Jordan, having fled Iraq because of the Invasion of Iraq in 2001. This activity helps to focus the learning on the impact that war has on civilians, particular children.

In the excerpts below, we learn of the dreams of young people who have experienced and suffered through war in their own countries. Ask the students:

- What do you learn about from the child's perspective?
- What can we do to make the world better for the child?
- What questions would you ask this young person?
- What do you think Deborah Ellis' intention was in collecting and publishing these stories?

Students can role-play an interview with a child of war, write a letter in role, or use an excerpt to read aloud as a monologue in role.

One of my dreams is to become very educated and very capable and to some day establish some sort of organization to take care of children who have suffered in war. Many have suffered much more than I have, but I have some understanding of what they go through, how they feel their world is taken away from them.
—Hibba, age 16

This was my house! This was my street! IT wasn't hurting anyone! It was just being a house. The place where I slept was now rocks and dust and chunks of roofs and walls. I think it would make the world better if people had to fix the things they broke.
—Michael, age 12

See page 139 for two sample letters from *The Globe and Mail* series.

In 2008, *The Globe and Mail* newspaper provided a series featuring the correspondence between a soldier and his wife during the time he was stationed in World War II. The two samples on page 139 share the horror of the experience as well as the deep love this soldier had for his wife. At the end of the series in the newspaper, readers learn that David did not survive the war.

Letters such as these can be a rich source for drama exploration, since they give us the inner thoughts of a real person. Not only can they be brought to life through theatre techniques, but they provide a springboard for role-play and writing in role.

Additional war letters and background information can be found on *The Globe and Mail* website: theglobeandmail.com/dearsweetheart

- Students are divided into pairs. One partner receives letter A (July 10, 1941), the others, letter B (March 7, 1942). To begin, students each have a chance to read the letter out loud. Partners can discuss what information they learn about these people from the letters.
- Students with the same letter join together. In groups of four, students prepare a theatrical presentation using these letters. Students need to decide which characters will be featured in the scene, where the letters will be read and/or written. Students should rehearse and direct the scene as if it were in a play. Each student needs to have a role in the scene. Students can share their prepared scenes and compare the different choices that each group made. Students can discuss: What did you learn about the people from the presentation of the letters? What did you learn this time and place?
- Students write in role, from the point of view of the soldier or his wife (or another family member). What letter might they have written any time in the years 1941 and 1942? Students should date the letter. Invite students to read aloud excerpts of the letter. You can decide whether these are to be read randomly, in chronological order, or grouped by character.

A Drama Structure Using a Picture Book

The Enemy: A book about peace by Davide Cali and Serge Bloch invites readers to consider what it means to be an enemy. In the picture book we are shown one battlefield. In that battlefield there are two holes. In each hole, a soldier sits, thinking about the enemy. What is forcing the enemy to remain in the hole? Which will be first to leave the hole? What steps can be taken to end the war? This book questions invites many questions about the reasons for war, the most important question being "Who is the Enemy?"

THINKING ABOUT WAR: BRAINSTORMING

Students were divided into four groups. Groups were given a chart, each with a different heading: *Movies, Songs, Books, Historical Events*. A time limit of five minutes was given for each group to brainstorm any titles that came to mind on the topic of war. Once completed, students did a walkabout and were invited to add titles that they thought could be included on each chart. Student volunteers explained some of the titles that might not have been familiar to the whole group.

A Soldier Writes Home

Thursday, July 10, 1941

Dear Sweetheart

I hope that you didn't think I was being too casual in my goodbye to you at the station. But you know how I hate a scene, and I didn't feel any too good myself so I had to say cheerio and run. But really and truly this was the worst yet. It was extremely hard to say anything to you or particularly the youngsters, and I am glad they aren't old enough to realize the uncertainty of this last goodbye.

The one important thing I want you to know is that I love you with all my heart, and that this love will not alter one bit no matter how long I am away.

Your job now is harder than mine in that you won't have definite knowledge of where I am. Please for my sake keep smiling, and above all don't worry.

I am not very good at saying these things on paper, but remember Tennyson's remarks on prayer, and that we believe in them. Above all remember that I love you and will always be thinking of you.

With all my love to you, Anne, Karen and Nanny,

I am always yours, David

Sussex, March 7, 1942

I realize that this war business is much harder on you than it is on me but that is just the condition that we must put up with… If all of us put our own little desires for new things and happy times now, ahead of our duty, we soon wouldn't have either freedom or liberty to enjoy anything…

Please don't read the above as a scolding or a lecture of any kind, but that is what we must keep in mind all the time. When I see pictures of youngsters in hospitals, all banged up from bombings, I can't help but feel that, until this menace is removed, the manpower of the entire Empire should be willing to undergo the sacrifice. It must be heartbreaking to have children turn to you for protection during an air raid and know that you are as helpless as they. That picture more than anything else makes me put up with being away from you and the girls.

I am always yours, David

Pembroke Publishers ©2010 *Drama Schemes, Themes & Dreams* by Larry Swartz and Debbie Nyman ISBN 978-1-55138-253-1

Students can respond to any picture book on the theme of war (see Recommended Resources on page 172).

See page 150 for an assessment rubric for Writing in Role.

WAR MONUMENTS: SCULPTING

Students worked in groups of four or five to create a monument in remembrance of war. The title "The Enemy" was assigned to the group. One group was assigned the role of the sculptor who was responsible for creating the monument out of the clay (i.e., each of the group members). In this trust exercise, the students, as clay, were required to be manipulated by the sculptor. Once the image had been created, sculptors were instructed to fit themselves into the monument.

Students then had the opportunity to be an audience for each other's work. Each group was assigned to present their monument in turn while the remainder of the class took a "walk through the park" where the monuments were displayed. As tourists, they commented on what they felt was depicted in the monument.

The students stood in a large circle. The students were invited to create a large monument by including ideas from each of the small monuments. When tapped on the shoulder, a student entered the space to create an image that he or she felt would be featured in the monument. Students were invited to consider levels, spacing, and balance as they collaboratively built the sculpture. Students could, if they wished, connect themselves to others.

The activity was repeated, this time with musical accompaniment.

DO YOU SEE WHAT I SEE?: RESPONDING TO *THE ENEMY*

In this activity, a graphic organizer was used to help students write a response after listening to the picture book, *The Enemy* by Davide Cali and Serge Bloch, being read out loud. Students had the opportunity to share their personal response with two friends and to consider similarities and differences of opinions.

A blank piece of paper was folded twice to make four rectangles; each space was numbered.

In space #1, students recorded their response to the picture book, considering what the book reminded them of, explaining their opinion, raising questions, or sharing their feelings in response to the book.

Students exchanged papers with another person in the group. Each student read the response that was recorded in space #1. Students then wrote in space #2, responding to what was written in #1. The activity was repeated by exchanging papers. Both responses on the sheet that was received were read. A third response was written in #3.

The sheet was returned to the person who wrote the first response. All three responses were considered and, in space #4, a new response was written: How had their thoughts been validated or altered by reading someone else's words?

In groups, students discussed the picture book collaboratively. Groups shared their responses in a whole-class discussion about the book *The Enemy*.

TOSSING A MESSAGE: WRITING IN ROLE

Students were given a piece of white paper on which to write a message in role. Using an image from the picture book, the scenario was established of two enemies, each hiding in their own hole, tossing a message to one another. The students were told to imagine that they were one of the enemies in one of the holes. To begin, each student wrote one sentence.

The students were arranged in two lines facing each other, Enemy Line A and Enemy Line B. On a signal, students crumpled their messages and tossed them into the centre space. Each student then picked up a new crumpled message, read it, and replied by adding one more sentence. The messages were crumpled up again and tossed into the centre. Again the students picked up a crumpled note, read it, and added one more sentence.

Students, in turn, read their three-sentence message out loud. The class discussed similarities and differences in the messages. A decision was made to have two enemies meet together.

THE ENEMIES MEET: FORUM THEATRE

The class negotiated and selected two letters to further explore through forum theatre. The two "enemies" (i.e., those who held the messages) were selected. The class came to a consensus about how the two enemies would meet, the distance between them, body language, setting, etc. The remaining students sat in a circle surrounding the enemies and the teacher explained that their role would be two-fold:

Students often get engaged in the forum. The teacher's role is to encourage students to be patient, to slow down and listen to each other, to build on each other's ideas. The forum might build the first few lines of the scene. Students are challenged to create an authentic moment that can be agreed upon.

1) to respond as audience, and
2) to create and direct the action and dialogue for the performers.

As the students worked, they continued to rewind, incorporating suggestions from the audience. As the improvisation unfolded, another option was to have students replace one of the actors to try out an option.

Extension

A possible extension of forum theatre would be to have students write a script that incorporates the dialogue and information begun in the forum scene.

CULMINATING ACTIVITY: SHOULD I GO? PAIRED IMPROVISATION

The enemy returns home to his family. Students worked in pairs to create an improvisation between the enemy and one of his children. The students were told that the son or daughter is thinking about enlisting. The parent and child had a conversation: What questions will the child ask? What information, stories, and advice will the parent offer?

Extension

This activity could be done using "secret information." Students were divided into A and B: A students were told that they are the parents; B students were the children. The children have asked the parents to meet them at a restaurant/café. The children were given secret information that they were going to inform their parent that they are going to enlist. Following the improvisation, students arranged themselves into inner circle (parents) and outer circle (children).

• Teacher asked children: How did it go with your father? How did this conversation help you to make a decision about war?
• Teacher asked parents: How do you feel about your child's decision? If you could say one more thing to your child, what might you reveal?

Artifacts could include

- Announcements
- Calendar of events
- Casualty lists
- Instruction manual
- Inventories
- Job description
- Letters, Maps, Menus
- List of rules/regulations
- Newspaper headlines/reports
- Notices of upcoming events
- Obituaries/eulogies, Wills
- Official reports to authorities
- Petitions, Résumés, Journals
- Photographs or illustrations (with labels/captions)
- Plans/blueprints
- Poems, Posters, Song lyrics
- Supplies lists, Work orders, "To do" lists

Extending the Drama

CREATING A WAR MUSEUM

The class decides as a group what items they think should be considered to be included in a war museum. Items in the museum might include drawings, posters, photographs, props, tape recordings, videos, a mural, dioramas, etc. This activity can be done in one of the following ways:

- Students work in groups as a committee who are planning the display for the war museum. Each group can report what they think might be included.
- Students can work in role as docents for a war museum. Students can work in pairs to guide a visitor through the museum. Since no items are on display, students can invent what the visitors will be seeing. Each partner should have the opportunity to be the docent guide.
- The students can work individually, in pairs, or in small groups to create the display by including art, writing, audio, and props. Another class could come to be the visitors for the museum. Students who prepared the museum can be docents explaining each of the items on display.

Digging Deep and Bearing Witness

by Jeanie Nishimura, educator, professional life coach

Drama is an art form based on the human capacity to be in the moment, experiencing and, at the same time, able to watch ourselves within the experience. We agree to "the willing suspension of disbelief" and enter the pretend as if it is real, all the while knowing it is not, stepping into role while at the same time watching ourselves playing the role. It is this heightened capacity that gives role playing such power as a learning medium. By inviting students into role, we are fostering their capacity to notice in the moment on multiple levels.

In working with many adolescents over my 28 years as a secondary drama teacher and consultant, and as a consultant and course instructor, I was consistently aware that role-playing pulls participants in to try on new experiences within imagined worlds and at the same time challenges all to notice and reflect. We enter imagined worlds and, using a variety of drama strategies, uncover the inherent human challenges within. The depth of experience and reflection is dependent upon engagement, willingness to co-create in the moment, and the capacity of the teacher and students to be curious and in awe of the complexities of the human condition. As teachers, we see how the power of role supports student engagement, discovery, and learning.

Finding compelling and rich contexts to explore with students is part of the magic of drama. Our invitations are always about heightening awareness and understanding by inhabiting role and observing. I remember inviting secondary students to set up an imagined scene within the fairytale of *Cinderella*, where Cinderella tries to approach her father for support, given the challenges she is facing in her relationships with her stepmother and stepsisters. The audience was invited to help Cinderella as she tried to get her father's attention and support. We explored the convention of forum theatre to help the protagonist garner strategies and behaviors that could truly change the outcome of the interactions. In role and out of role, the students stopped the scene for reflection and strategizing, and then invited Cinderella, with her expanded awareness, to try again to get the help she needs as a daughter. The depth of the emerging awareness of the challenges within the family relationships and dynamic was palpable within the classroom.

Another invitation to dig deep and bear witness that I vividly remember was in a Grade 10 drama class. I began by posting an evocative quotation taken from the John LeCarre novel, *Russia House*: "The knight is dying inside his armor. …Believe me." I then invited the students, in pairs, to explore possible modern-day contexts that might be represented by these words. Lots of engagement and energy was evident in the room, as students brainstormed possibilities. As teacher, I was circulating, asking clarifying questions of each pair, challenging them to dig deeper as they built their context and explored the resonance of the quote. Two boys had settled on an image of a dead soldier with an ID tag, accompanied by his bereft colleague and friend. I asked them what war they were fighting in; they hadn't considered that yet. I stood with them, asking further questions that pushed them to reflect more deeply on war, death, and the implications of their interpretation of the quotation. Deciding it was the Vietnam War and they were American soldiers in a war they no longer believed in, they became much more animated and engaged, asking further questions of themselves as they reshaped their image to reflect their gathering wisdom and deepening understanding.

It is my belief that these moments of deepening engagement and emotional resonance are the essence of learning and growing through drama. Standing in someone else's shoes invites us to think and feel as that person and notice the awareness it brings to ourselves as well as to those bearing witness. Drama allows us to imagine as if we are another and, when we introduce work that invites students to work in role, we are helping them to participate in other points of view so that they can better understand their own. Following the events of September 11, 2001, Ian McEwan wrote in an article in *The Guardian* newspaper, "Imagining what it is like to be someone other than yourself is at the core of our humanity. It is the essence of compassion, and it is the beginning of morality."

Script Variation: War in Word and Song

FROM DIARY ENTRIES TO MONOLOGUES

One single Anne Frank moves us more than the countless others who suffered just as she did, but whose faces have remained in the shadows.

—Primo Levi

Students independently read a picture book on the theme of war. Have each student imagine that he or she is a character in this story who is writing a diary to describe his or her feelings about war. This entry can be written before, during, or after the direct war experience. Alternatively, students can write a letter in role to someone who is involved in a war.

Once completed, students work in pairs to exchange writing-in-role pieces. Students are given an opportunity to interview one another. Students can work in role to interview each other. Students can also "assign" the reader a role: Who might be reading the diary/letter?

Because they are written in the first person, the writing-in-role samples can be used as monologues for the students to perform for others. Students can rehearse their script, but are encouraged to tell the story that this person would tell others. Students can consider the use of props and simple costumes for their monologue presentations. How will they stand or sit? What gestures and actions will they add to their monologue presentations?

WAR POEMS

See Strategy Scheme: Ten Ways to Read a Poem Out Loud on page 62

The poems on page 145 can be used for choral dramatization. Because these poems are rather short, students can work in groups of 2 or 3 to explore ways to read them aloud together. Encourage the students to consider an effective way to begin and end their choral dramatization.

Extension

Students choose any two poems. They are challenged to weave the two poems together. The easiest strategy is to take one line from each poem and read the lines, alternating between poems. Students can, however, divide lines into segments, repeat lines, or rearrange the order. Students can then work together to present the poem chorally, including simple gesture and movement.

Before me peaceful
Let there be peace on earth

Behind me
    Let it begin with me
Peaceful
    Let there be peace on earth
Under me peaceful
    And let it begin in my heart
Over me peaceful
    Let there be miracles on earth
    And let them begin with my faith
    Let there be a future
Around me peaceful.
    NOW!

SONGS ABOUT WAR

A list of songs have been provided in the Recommended Resources list on page 173.

Often the lyrics for songs can provide strong sources for drama exploration. Songs can also be

- sung by individuals, in groups, or by the whole class.
- used as transitions between scenes
- read aloud as choral dramatization
- used as a background for tableaux, movement, or dance drama work
- created by the students; i.e., changing the words, adding a verse

RESPONDING TO A POEM

Fantasia
I dream
of
giving birth
to
a child
who will ask,
"Mother,
What was war?"
—Eve Merriam

Present students with the poem by Eve Merriam. Students work in groups of four. The placemat strategy is used by students to respond to the poem. Students are each assigned a space in the placemat graphic organizer to record their responses to the poem. The following prompts were used to consider the message behind the poem:

- What does the title "Fantasia" make you think about?
- Is it possible for this mother's dream to ever come true?
- Why do we have wars?

Students share their responses and, as a group, synthesize their ideas to write a response in the centre that consolidates and represents the group's thinking. A spokesperson from each group represents the group by reading the collaborative written response and explaining how the group came to that thinking.

War Poems

The grand old Duke of York
He had ten thousand men
He marched them up to the top of the
   hill
And he marched them down again.
And when they were up, they were up
And when they were down, they were
   down
But when they were only halfway up
They were neither up nor down.

Before me peaceful,
Behind me peaceful,
Under me peaceful,
Over me peaceful,
Around me peaceful.

                        Navajo Prayer

Let there be peace on earth
Let it begin with me
Let there be peace on earth
And let it begin in my heart
Let there be miracles on earth
And let them begin with my faith
Let there be a future
And let it begin with my action –
NOW!

                        Anon

Deep peace of the Running Wave to you
Deep peace of Flowing Air to you
Deep peace of the Quiet Earth to you
Deep peace of the Shining Stars to you
Deep peace of the Gentle Night to you
Deep Peace of the Son of Peace to you
Moon and stars pour their healing light
   on you
Deep peace to you

                        Celtic blessing

I hate and I love.
And if you ask me how,
I do not know: I only feel it,
and I'm torn in two.

                        Catullus

For want of a nail the shoe was lost.
For want of a shoe the horse was lost.
For want of a horse the rider was lost.
For want of a rider the battle was lost.
For want of a battle the kingdom was
   lost.
And all for the want of a horseshoe
   nail.

                        Anon

Students are asked to write one sentence that a mother (or father) might use to answer the child's question from the poem. The following prompts could be used:

- *Child, I...*
- *My son/My daughter,...*
- *My dream...*

Students share their responses, with each person in turn reading aloud, speaking in role of the parent.

Students transform their one-sentence answers to create a free verse poem. By writing one, two, or three words on a line, and considering white spaces, the students can create a poem that tells the answer to the child's question.

My child, there was once a time when we lost
our humanity and the world was broken.

My child
There was once at time when
we lost
our humanity
and the world was
broken.

Illustrating the Poem

Tell students to imagine that this poem is going to appear in an illustrated poetry anthology. Students can create a visual image (realistic or abstract) that could accompany the poem.

Strategy Scheme: The Collective Creation

One of the most useful ways to build a Collective Creation or the school assembly is to integrate a variety of strategies that have been explored in a unit of work. The ideas presented throughout this drama theme on the topic of war can be developed from classroom process to performance. The outline below offers suggestions of dramatic forms that can be utilized. The order of presenting this work, the transitions from scene to scene, and the use of props, lights, and music can help to enrich the experience for the audience.

Here is an outline of procedures to rehearse and present a Collective Creation:

1. Negotiate and select with the students the scenes, materials, activities from the unit that they wish to take to presentation.
2. Students decide which of the events they would like to rehearse. Students can commit themselves to working with a partner or in small groups to explore the work. Some students may choose to rehearse a solo piece. Decisions will need to be made for students to present as a whole group (choral presentation, movement piece, etc.)
3. Groups revise and edit the scenes to discover new meaning. At this stage they will need to consider preparing the piece for an audience; i.e., sight lines, voice work, pacing, etc.

4. Rehearsal time should be given where groups share their work with the class. Encourage the students to give each other constructive feedback to polish the work.

5. Decisions need to be made for negotiating a sequence: Is there a natural order? Is there variety in the types of work that will be presented in sequence? Is there one scene that will be a strong opening? A strong conclusion?

6. Students link the pieces together in a meaningful way. Transitions need to create a sense of continuity, coherency, and clarity to help make thematic connections.

7. Students can consider use of props, costumes, music. If available, lighting can enhance the presentation.

8. As a group consider these issues: Who is the audience? What is the size of the audience? What is the appropriate space for presentation?

9. A final dress rehearsal should ensure that students are familiar with their parts, their cues, the transitions, and their responsibility to the group—and the work.

10. Students perform the Collective Creation.

Reflection

- What did you learn about theatre as a means of communication?
- What did you enjoy about working on a collective creation? What were some challenges you encountered?
- How successfully do you think you contributed to the work?
- What changes might you make if you were to perform the work again?
- What new understandings do you think the audience took away with them?

THE REMEMBRANCE DAY ASSEMBLY: A SUGGESTED OUTLINE

1. **Choral dramatization (whole group):** "Prayer for the 21st Century" by John Marsden

2. **Choral dramatization (small group):** War poems (see page 143); Student-written poems (see page 146)

3. **Monologues:** Letters (see page 138); Students' in-role diaries (see page 143); The Children of War (see page 137)

4. **Movement:** The Wave (see page 136)

5. **Dance Drama:** War Monuments (see page 140)

6. **Songs:** "Earth Song" (Michael Jackson); "Imagine" (John Lennon)

7. **Media:** Video or projections of photographs

8. **Improvised Scenes:** The Enemies Meet (see page 141); Should I Go? (see page 141)

9. **Script excerpt:** *War Horse, Billy Bishop Goes to War*

10. **Tableaux:** Photographs (see page 135)

From Page to Stage: The Joys and Challenges of Student Performance

by Kathleen Fraumeni former principal, London District Catholic School Board

The teacher stood at the front of our class and began to turn the pages, reading aloud from Dickens' *Great Expectations*. Her words cut across centuries, and she spoke no longer as narrator but in the voice of young boy caught in bleak world of a time gone by. I was no longer seated in a classroom, but, with each passage that she read, was pulled deeper into the world of Pip, terrified of the convict that lurked around every corner. From that moment, I was forever a reader and forever a believer in the power of drama as a tool for learning. Teachers can provide those powerful links for students between the words on the page and a clearer understanding of story and characters by taking the learning into the realm of role-play, drama, and theatre.

Opportunities abound within the curriculum for elementary students and their teachers to bring stories, poetry, scripts, and student writing to life in the classroom and in school auditoriums. The process involves a teacher with a vision and a group of students enthusiastic enough to give the characters a voice to tell the story to an eager audience. But lifting the story *from page to stage* in an elementary school is not for the faint of heart!

The literary and creative process begins when the teacher and the students make a connection to a story or poem that begs to be transformed into art. The vision is one of a script or perhaps a dance that will tell the story, enhanced by artwork to create the backdrop and by children who will work collaboratively and creatively. The subject of the performance may be a Shel Silverstein poem, a well-loved fairy tale, or even an original piece of student writing with a message worthy of performing for others. It may be a published script or musical that needs to be leased or purchased by the school in order to be produced. Teachers will find that there are many publishing houses and Internet sources for very kid-friendly scripts, available with and without royalty costs. Some teachers may choose to write their own script or have students write the script, feeling that the dialogue or narration would then be more suited and accessible to the needs of their students. Ultimately, the teacher will choose a script that is age-appropriate for the children and substantially linked to the curriculum learning expectations for literacy and the arts.

There is great courage involved on the part of the teacher who chooses to stage a production, large or small. It is a commitment of time, talent, and energy, with an ultimate goal to enrich the learning experience of the students. The teacher becomes director, producer, and, depending on the choice of script, conductor and choreographer! The most successful school productions are those that call on the talents of many staff members, students, and parents. It is wise to identify the support in the school at a very early stage of planning, so that all staff members, including the principal, are aware of the scope of the production, the timeline, and the tasks that will be involved. Similarly, parents are tremendous allies in a production, since they represent a vast array of talents as carpenters, painters, and costume designers. In most cases, parents and guardians are more than happy, if they are able, to support their child's arts experience.

Once the subject and script have been chosen and royalties (if required) have been secured, decisions are made in terms of performers. Some schools ask children to audition to play certain characters. Other schools tap the performers on the shoulder (especially in the primary grades), or even have a few students share a role, alternating the performances for different audiences. In many cases, teachers choose to stage choral works, in which all the children speak, sing, or dance the performance as an ensemble. No one is left out and each child shines in the process. The more traditional "school play" has a cast of actors chosen for their strengths in role play and their ability to portray the characters in a meaningful way. Dealing with the disappointment of students and parents when one child is chosen over another can be a challenge for the teacher. The message that is most helpful to students and parents from the outset is that each child contributes an essential element of creativity to the stage production, whether as someone who speaks or sings a few lines or as a member of the larger chorus. The creative process involved in bringing the work to the stage must always be the focus of the project rather than the performance itself.

The cast is in place, the support crew is hard at work, and the rehearsal schedule is posted and shared with parents. Much of the preparation for the production can take place in class time, with careful planning on the part of the teacher and with the integration of the arts at many points across the curriculum. Visual arts skills can be used in creating backdrops and/or props. Drama skills, such as role play, creative movement, and dance, can be nicely refined through literacy learning, enhancing students' ability to portray characters more effectively. Choral musical numbers can be learned in class time, while students with solo pieces will need one-on-one assistance in a designated rehearsal time. As a result of these important curriculum links to music, visual arts, drama, and dance, the students will feel confident and better prepared to follow direction during rehearsals for their productions.

Whether the final production is a student version of *Great Expectations* presented in class to peers or a musical production presented to an audience of parents and the community, it will be the creative process that the students will remember. They will benefit from the careful planning of their teacher, who incorporated visual arts, music, drama, and dance into their everyday learning, making them capable learners in communicating their ideas to an audience with purpose, creativity, and meaning. The teacher will recall the collaboration, the benefits of networking with staff and parents, and the thrill of seeing an artistic vision transfer *from page to stage*.

Assessment: Rubric for Writing in Role

Criteria	Level 1	Level 2	Level 3	Level 4
Understands the role and imagined context	Limited understanding of character's point of view and circumstances of the drama	Some understanding of character's point of view and circumstances of the drama	Considerable understanding of character's point of view and circumstances of the drama	Deep and thorough understanding of character's point of view and circumstances of the drama
Reflects on the learning through the writing	Limited understanding of themes and issues in the drama; makes limited connections to themes, topics, or issues	Some understanding of themes and issues in the drama; makes some connections to themes, topics, or issues	Understanding of themes and issues in the drama is insightful and detailed; makes meaningful connections to themes, topics, or issues	Understanding of themes and issues in the drama is insightful and very detailed; makes meaningful and thoughtful connections to themes, topics, or issues
Communicates with purpose and clarity	Communicates character's thoughts and feelings through limited use of format, language, and conventions	Communicates character's thoughts and feelings through satisfactory use of format, language, and conventions	Communicates character's thoughts and feelings through effective use of format, language, and conventions	Communicates character's thoughts and feelings through highly effective use of format, language, and conventions
Demonstrates awareness of audience	Limited understanding of the context, function, and intended audience of the piece	Satisfactory understanding of the context, function, and intended audience of the piece	Good understanding of the context, function, and intended audience of the piece	Excellent understanding of the context, function, and intended audience of the piece

Pembroke Publishers ©2010 *Drama Schemes, Themes & Dreams* by Larry Swartz and Debbie Nyman ISBN 978-1-55138-253-1

Dreams Aloud

To die, to sleep;
To sleep: perchance to dream: aye, there's the rub.
—William Shakespeare, *Hamlet*, Act 111, scene i

Drama Theme: Dreams

Any of the plays that we see, whether dramas, comedies, musicals, or otherwise, have an element of dreams within them: dreams about love, hope, change, coping, determination, goal-reaching, survival, reverie. Often dreams are the core of many classic drama characters—Willy Loman in *Death of a Salesman* by Arthur Miller, Laura in *The Glass Menagerie* by Tennessee Williams, and Walter Lee in *Raisin in the Sun* by Lorraine Hansberry. In a number of musicals, characters burst out in song about dreams: "I Have Dreamed" (*The King and I*), "The Impossible Dream" (*Man of LaMancha*), "I Have a Dream" (*Mamma Mia*), and "Any Dream Will Do" (*Joseph and the Amazing Technicolor Dreamcoat*).

This unit offers students experiences with a number of script sources, including one-liners, minimal scripts, dialogue scripts, scenes, and monologues. The word "dream" may not appear in the text but, by lifting the words off the page through voice and gesture, students investigate possibilities that emerge on, off, and between the lines of a script. As students interpret, improvise, rehearse, and present scripts, they can discover how each of the characters communicate their thoughts, feelings—and dreams. One of the best ways to come to understand a character is to uncover and discover his or her dreams.

LEARNING OPPORTUNITIES

- To practice mime skills by communicating situations nonverbally
- To enrich the archetypal understanding of dreams by connecting with the characters presented in plays
- To experiment with a number of ways to read lines out loud
- To bring meaning to one-liners and minimal scripts by considering possibilities of character, place, and intention for interpreting lines
- To negotiate with others meaningful ways to interpret scripts in order to realize a playwright's intention
- To interpret monologue scripts, and to develop scenes that include characters suggested by the monologue

- To explore ways of revising and rehearsing a script to present scenes to an audience
- To write scripted scenes and work with others to perform them
- To work with skills of directing script scenes from page to stage by considering voice, movement, gesture, staging, costume, props

Launching the Drama: Working without Words

Mime Workshop
by Naomi Tyrrell, mime and mask performer

I love mime. I discovered it when I was a teenager in a theatre school. When I realized that I could be anyone I wanted and go any place I pleased and eat all my favorite foods and not gain a pound, I was sold. I never left mime from that day on. I've been lucky enough to travel and teach all over the world, and one of the most wonderful things about this magical art form is that there is no language barrier. This workshop is designed to teach some simple mime skills, starting with the hands and face, moving to full-body illusion, and, lastly, adding character. Remember—exaggerate: open your eyes wide, let your face be like a cartoon character, and move slowly and deliberately for clarity. I find all ages love doing mime, from preschoolers right through to teachers and executives. I have so much more to say about how this art form has challenged me and shaped the person and performer that I am, but I am at a loss for words.

1. Butterfly

Attach your thumb and index finger together, spread all the other fingers out for the beautiful wings. Shake it about, look at it with hungry eyes, pop it in your mouth and eat it (chew lightly on your tongue and have it protrude out of your cheek for the illusion of eating something), swallow. Your stomach starts to shake; tap your belly and out it comes, grab it and throw it up in the air, and shake your head as you watch it fly away.

2. Baby Bird Hatching Out of an Egg

Cup your hands together to create an egg. Open your hands a little at a time until the egg is fully open. Cross your fingertips to create a baby bird; it gets bigger and bigger until your wrists are attached and the bird is fully grown. Create a wave in your hands for the wings; it tries to fly up and flutters back down, it tries twice more and succeeds on the third try. Open your arms wide and let them come down slowly as you watch it take its first flight.

3. Pesky Snake

Create a snake head by putting your thumb under your fingers; let it lead your arm as it slithers out from behind your back. Open the jaw and let the index finger quiver to play the tongue. The snake slithers up beside your face and you look at it with a frightened expression; push its head away and it comes back as if it's on a spring; repeat; the last time it bites your nose, you look terrified, yank it three times, and finally get it off.

It slithers away and you look relieved.

4. Expression Masks

Practice changing your expression by picking up an imaginary mask. Cover your face with your hand and remove your hand to reveal a series of expressions. Try these emotions one at a time and then add some of your own: happy, sad, surprised, angry, scared, silly.

5. The Wall

Place two hands flat on an imaginary vertical surface, take one away and curve it, then replace it; now do the other one; repeat, remembering to spread your fingers; only move one hand at a time and keep your eyes on the wall.

6. Jekyll and Hyde

Play the mad scientist with a crooked old back and wild eyes. Put on your lab coat, polish your wire-frame glasses, get your dusty old potion book, mix three ingredients (some may explode when mixed, some may try to hop away, and some may be smelly); hold up potion and repeat, *Over the teeth, over the gums, look out stomach, here it comes.* Drink it down and take a minute to make a complete physical transition; flip, flail, and shudder until you turn into a hideous, nasty monster.

7. This Is a Scarf

Students sit in a circle. An object is introduced to the group, a scarf, for example. Each student in turn is to perform a nonverbal activity that uses the scarf in some way to show what the scarf has become. As each person receives the scarf, he or she says, "This is a scarf, but it's not really a scarf, it's a _____." The scarf is passed around the circle until each player has had an opportunity to create a mime activity. The activity is repeated, but students are challenged not to duplicate anything that has been presented. Note: It is important that the students, as audience, follow the instruction to remain silent. Students may be excited and call out guesses as to what the object has become, but the performer should be encouraged to complete the mime activity with clarity.

Extensions

a) The object can be changed (e.g., a pencil, a belt, a ribbon, etc.).
b) Students pass an invisible object; e.g., a lump of clay that can be molded into anything.
c) This mime game can be played in pairs or in small groups.
d) Students can add a line of dialogue as they "use" the object.
e) Students can work in pairs or groups of three to improvise a scene using the object.

Framing the Theme: Short Scenes

EXPLORING MINIMAL SCRIPTS

See Minimal Scripts on page 155.

Minimal scripts are a good place for students to explore the fundamental elements of good theatre:

- WHO are the characters? What is their relationship to each other?
- WHAT is happening in the scene? What is the story?
- WHERE is the setting/location for the scene?
- WHEN is this scene taking place? time of day? season?
- WHY are these characters having a conversation? What are the character's objectives? motivations? dilemmas?
- HOW do the characters convey the mood and intent through voice, movement, and gesture?

Students work in pairs; in each pair, one partner takes the role of A, the second the role of B. As the directions are called out, partners practice saying the lines of script out loud. The pairs can practice saying the minimal scripts in a variety of ways. As the activity unfolds, it is important to switch up the partners who begin reading the lines.

- Say the lines as written.
- Reverse roles.
- Say the lines in a whisper.
- Say the lines as if talking on a telephone.
- One person says the lines angrily; the other, calmly.
- Both partners say the lines angrily.

- Speak while playing a clapping game.
- Partners echo each other's lines.
- Pause for a few seconds between lines.
- Sing the lines.
- Say the lines quickly.
- Shake hands.
- Make no eye contact.
- Stare at each other.
- Sit back-to-back.
- Shout across the room.
- One partner shows no interest in the conversation.

Extensions

a) Students can prepare a short improvisation incorporating the dialogue while performing an activity: e.g., reading a book, playing with blocks, working at a computer, getting dressed, preparing breakfast, making a pizza, doing exercises.
b) Students continue the conversations by adding to the dialogue for a short improvisation.
c) Students use the minimal scripts to end a conversation, rather than to begin one.
d) Students write short scripts by adding lines of dialogue to a minimal script. Pairs exchange scripts and prepare them for each other.
e) Instead of working in pairs, students work in groups of three or four. The conversation/improvisation changes when more than two people are involved.

ON THE LINE

Students work in partners A and B, and form two circles, with A partners facing B partners. The teacher gives the A partners an opening line for an improvisation: e.g., "I had a crazy dream last night," or "Are you daydreaming?" The A partners decide how to deliver the line and, on a signal from the teacher, A delivers the line; B responds, and together they build a brief scene. On a signal from the teacher, the students freeze and together remember the last line of their scene.

The A partners move two students to their right and the B circle does not move. With new partners, the B partners begin the improvisation with the last line of the previous improvisation. On a signal from the teacher, the pairs freeze and together remember the last line of the scene. The activity continues each time with new partners by moving the A or B circle.

The context is new with each new scene. The teacher can give specific "stage directions" to the students delivering the lines: e.g., delivering the line in a different physical position, with an emotion, making eye contact, repeating the line, etc.

THREE-WORD SCENES

Students work in groups of three. Each group is given the same three words; e.g., *Why/Sorry/Oh*. Triads create a scene using only those three words in any order. Students have to consider: What gestures, movements, and positions will they take to show the relationship of the characters and to bring meaning to the scene?

Three-Word Possibilities

So/Me/Thanks
No/Yes/Maybe
Perhaps/Sure/Never
Delicious/Please/Whatever
Absolutely/Awesome/Yuck

Minimal Scripts

Are you all right?
Why are you asking?

See you again?
Sure.
Really?
Perhaps.

Where are you going?
Out?
What do mean, "out"?
You worry too much.

What are you doing here?
Don't you know?
Should I?
You sent me the message.

Does he love her?
Yes.
Does she know it?
Yes.
Will he leave her?

I've got a secret.
Tell me.
I'm not sure.
I won't tell anybody here.

Haven't I seen you somewhere before?
I don't think so.
You don't remember?
Should I?
Forget it.

Pembroke Publishers ©2010 *Drama Schemes, Themes & Dreams* by Larry Swartz and Debbie Nyman ISBN 978-1-55138-253-1

Extensions

a) The students are challenged to experiment with the order of the three words to create two new scenes using only those three words. They may repeat the words. Which are their favorite scenes? Students can share the scenes and discuss the variety of interpretations.

DREAM STEMS INTO SCRIPTS

The Dream Stems below can be distributed to students. Alternatively, stems can be displayed on a chart and students work independently to copy and complete statements that feature the word "dream." Students do not write their names on their papers. Remind students that statements will be shared in a public way and that they should be comfortable with the responses they choose to share.

Dream Stems

I dream of becoming_____

In a dream I travel to_____

Sometimes I dream about_____

_____is my dream for you.

When I was little I would dream about _____

_____is the color of my dreams because_____

Once statements are completed, students walk through the space and read their pieces aloud, beginning anywhere but the top of the page to avoid reading in unison. On a signal from the teacher, students trade papers with as many other students as possible in 30 seconds. Students walk through the space reading their new dream statements. They walk beside a partner and share a line that they are intrigued by; with a new partner, sharing a line that is similar to one they wrote. On a signal from the teacher, students freeze and, when the teacher taps them on the shoulder, they read one of those choices aloud to the class. Students then trade papers again with as many students as possible in 30 seconds. Again they explore the new papers, reading aloud, sharing a line that made them smile, that made them sad. Students trade papers again, each time ensuring that they have a new set of statements.

After the students have read through the pieces aloud, they select one line that they connect to. Working alone, they memorize and create a physical shape to represent the line. On a signal from the teacher, students build a group image of "Dreams" by, one at a time, entering the space, creating the shape, and saying the line. Encourage students to connect their shapes and lines as they build the image together.

Reflection

- How did this activity help you to think about dreams?
- How did you feel hearing your line said aloud? Was it interpreted the way you intended? Did the other student's interpretation give it new meaning?
- What impression of dreams was communicated in the group piece?

We are such stuff
As dreams are made on, and our
    little life
Is rounded with sleep.
—William Shakespeare, *The Tempest*,
Act IV, Scene i

Strategy Scheme: Revising, Reshaping, and Rehearsing Scenes

These activities encourage students to explore, experiment, revise, and reshape script work from a better-informed place. This Strategy Scheme can be a starting point for teachers who direct extracurricular performances. The goal is to not only deepen the interpretation, but also to be successful in creating a strong piece of theatre for an audience.

- Read in a variety of ways vocally, changing tempo, volume, emotion, or attitude: e.g., quickly, slowly, loudly, softly, whispering, shouting.
- Alternate roles on signal from the teacher.
- Read in a variety of physical formations: sitting back-to-back, standing, lying down and looking at the ceiling, walking beside each other, walking one behind the other and turning each time to say the line.
- Read the script facing each other and making eye contact for the delivery of each line; i.e., look down at the script, retrieve the line, make eye contact, and then say the line.
- Read the script avoiding eye contact.
- Rehearse a scene beginning in a variety of places: halfway through, from the end to the beginning, forward and then backward.
- Rehearse the scene in a variety of settings: in a shopping mall, at a baseball game, in an aerobics class, at an Internet café, while rock climbing, while on a boat, etc.
- Rehearse the scene while doing a variety of activities: watching television, working out, doing homework, cleaning your room, dancing
- Have the character who delivers the first line walking ahead of his or her partner. The partner behind is always trying to catch up and the partner ahead is always trying to stay ahead. Reverse roles.
- Rehearse the scene, reducing each line to the most significant word and using only those words to communicate the meaning of the script.
- Play the scene with one physical action throughout. This may be mimed at first, but then try it with an actual physical not-mimed activity.
- Students choose or are given a prop to incorporate throughout the scene in a variety of ways.
- Before memorization, set aside the scripts and improvise the scene. Examine what was left out of the improvisation. Does this material need to be better internalized and understood?
- Rehearse without any dialogue, in order to develop concentration on the physical actions in the scene.
- Since beginnings are important, a physical action can be rehearsed for before the spoken lines. What physical action can be prepared for after the last line is said?
- Introduce a non-speaking role into the scene.

After working through Exploring Minimal Scripts on page 153, students can use the drama experiences to create scene scripts to revise, reshape, and rehearse. Students can develop scripts in the following ways:

a) Write a monologue from their character's point of view.
b) Write a script that shows some future time in the lives of these characters.
c) Write scenes using only these two characters; or featuring a different character.

d) Write in role: e.g., one character has returned to Canada and the two characters continue their relationship through e-mails one year later; five years later.

A Drama Structure Using Monologue Script

The following drama structure encourages students to look inside and outside a short piece of text. The activities described below can be used to introduce the students to monologue scripts or monologue excerpts. Often these voices provide possibilities of uncovering stories within the story. Because a problem or dilemma is suggested, these excerpts are particularly useful for connecting interpretation and improvisation activities.

A Drama Scheme Guaranteed to Work

Set the Scene	• to build interest and establish a context as well as access prior knowledge or experience (e.g. a game, personal narrative, drama activity)
Interpret	• to bring meaning to the words through voice
Discuss	• to make predictions, hypothesize, and make connections
Question	• to build commitment and explore puzzles
Interview	• to work in role, to find answers, to tell stories, and to build character
Improvise	• to depict events from a character's life
Conduct a Meeting	• to negotiate meaning and/or to solve problems
Extend	• to dig deeper into the drama, to write in role, to present drama work

WHAT I DON'T KNOW ABOUT YOU: MENTAL SET/PERSONAL NARRATIVE

Students worked in pairs and were provided with a list of items. Each partner chose one item from the list as a topic to ask about. To begin, Partner A said, "What I don't know about you is [topic]," and partner B answered, telling a personal narrative connected to that topic. Partner B then chose a topic and asked A.

Next, students chose three items from the list and offered these three topics to a partner. The partner chose one topic to answer. The game was repeated with each person alternatively introducing different topics.

Topics included:

- siblings
- your best vacation
- your favorite book
- your favorite kind of music

- where you were born
- what is important about your name
- your allergies
- if you have had any accidents/stitches
- places you've moved to

ACT ONE, SCENE ONE: MEETING THE MONOLOGUE

I have a little brother.

His name is Alphonse.

He's a brave kid, Alphonse: his green eyes look right at you. When he walks down the street, people don't notice him. He doesn't want anyone to notice him. Anyway, he's just not the kind of kid people notice.

Tonight Alphonse didn't come home from school. My mother's sitting in the living room, her knitting beside her.

My father's smoking by the wide-open window staring into the night, my sister's asleep (actually she's pretending).

And me, I'm sitting in the kitchen, worrying about Alphonse. Where the hell can he be? The little weasel.

—from *Alphonse* by Wajdi Mouawad (translated by Shelley Tepperman)

Students examined the script to determine the following:

- Which characters do we learn about in this monologue?
- Where does the action take place?
- What is the longest line of dialogue? The shortest?
- What problem is introduced in the opening scene?
- What stage directions are provided to give the reader information about performing the scene?
- What predictions can you make about future scenes?
- When this scene is performed on stage, how do you visualize the set? What do you think the costumes look like?

MONOLOGUE ALOUD: INTERPRETATION

Students were arranged in groups of six to eight to read the monologue in the following ways:

- The group reads the monologue in unison.
- One person begins reading the monologue from beginning to end. When he or she has completed two sentences, the person on the right begins to read the monologue from beginning to end. The activity continues so that the monologue is read as a round.
- One person is assigned to begin reading. He or she reads only one sentence of the monologue. The reading continues through the group, with each person reading one sentence at a time. Continue until the monologue has been completed.
- Repeat the above activity. This time, the reader is challenged to read only the most important group of words from the sentence, as if taking a high-lighter marker to the text.
- Repeat the above activity. Each reader chooses one word to read from the assigned sentence.

HERE'S WHAT I THINK: DISCUSSION

The group discussed what information they learned from the opening scene by considering the following:

- Why might the character be saying these lines?
- What is the story?
- What other characters might we learn about by continuing to read the play?
- Does this monologue remind them of events from their own lives? From other books, movies or plays they have experienced?

I WONDER...: QUESTIONING

Students in groups of four or five were allowed 15 minutes to brainstorm a list of questions on chart paper that they would ask this character if he or she came into the room. Once the questions were completed, groups reviewed questions to designate the following:

- Which question(s) requires an answer of Yes or No?
- Which question(s) is not particularly relevant?
- Which two questions are the most significant?

Groups shared their key questions, which were recorded on a chart.

DO YOU MIND IF I ASK YOU SOME QUESTIONS? INTERVIEWING IN ROLE/HOT-SEATING

The class suggested names of characters that they could interview to learn more about the story, the problem, and the relationships connected to this character; e.g., siblings, classmate, neighbor, teacher.

Students volunteered to take on a role of one of these characters. Using hot seating, each of the characters in turn was interviewed by the group.

Following the interviews, students returned to their list of questions: What questions from their original list have been answered? What new questions do we have?

WHAT WE DON'T KNOW ABOUT: PERSONAL NARRATIVE IN ROLE

For this activity, the character of Alphonse is *not* introduced.

Students were introduced to the character of Alphonse, played by the teacher. The students replayed the personal narrative activity What I Don't Know About You (see page 158) and the teacher in role told stories to give new information about the character. Individual students offered two or three topics to present to Alphonse, and teacher in role chose one that would bring the most authenticity to the situation.

THE PLAY OF MY LIFE: SMALL-GROUP IMPROVISATION

Students worked in pairs to create a scene to show an episode from Alphonse's life that might explain why he chose to leave, or that might provide a clue of where Alphonse might be. The short scene (two to three minutes) could feature any two characters.

BUILDING SCRIPT FROM IMPROVISATION

Students prepared scripted scenes using dialogue and information from their improvisation. The scene needed to involve three characters, including Alphonse. Pairs exchanged scripts to interpret scripts that were not their own.

CULMINATING ACTIVITY: *ALPHONSE: THE PLAY*

Each group in turn presented their rehearsed scenes to create a play of *Alphonse*. This provided students the opportunity to invent and script multi-character scenes for a monologue play.

Reflection

- How did you feel listening your script performed by others? What did you learn from watching the script being performed by others?
- What changes might you suggest to achieve better theatre?
- How do writing and presenting these scenes with many characters help you to further understand the identity of the characters?
- What are the challenges for an actor to perform a monologue?

Extending the Drama

Writing Monologues

Students can write a monologue from the point of view of a character met in the improvisation. Students can rehearse and work toward presenting monologue scenes to others.

Writing in Role

After improvising scenes that feature this character, students can create a diary entry that would reveal the character's thoughts and feelings. These entries could be transformed into monologues to be rehearsed and presented.

Further Interpretation

Provide students with other scenes from the script. Students can work in groups to rehearse and present these scenes. What new information do we learn in these scenes? Have your predictions been confirmed?

Illustrating the Set

Students can illustrate a set design that could be used for the opening scene.

Designing a Poster

Using information from Act One, Scene One (see page 159), students design a poster that could be used to advertise the play.

Mime

Challenge students to create the opening monologue without using any words.

Script Variation: Interpreting Scenes

UNPACKING A SCENE

These activities can be centred on the play *Rice Boy* by Sunil Kuruvilla. See excerpts of script on page 163.

Students in a drama class are always asking the teacher, "When do we get our scripts?" They come to our classes with an understanding of theatre that a play begins with a script.

In our work together, we build many plays and scripts from poetry and prose, stories and images, and our students become committed to those scripts and they see them as meaningful. However, it is important, in working in the art form of theatre, that we do take them inside the formalized script, that we help them discover the meaning and become committed and connected to the characters. We can work on one scene together; we can work in groups and explore different scenes; we can explore different scenes from one play from a variety of genres, periods, places in the world. Our students are student actors, working in the art form with us as guides. We create the opportunities for them to question, to wrestle with the tension and conflict, to find the authentic voices of the characters, and to communicate those voices and moments with integrity and significance. Together, working from the inside, we unpack the scene and share out understandings with each other and the audience.

You can provide students with additional scenes from the play for this interpretation activity. Encourage students to read the pay in its entirety to learn more about the characters.

In the play *Rice Boy* we are introduced to a 17-year-old Indian girl named Tina, a paraplegic who is awaiting an arranged marriage to a man she has never met. Tommy, a cousin from Canada, visits her, and we learn about his life as an immigrant in a rural community. Tommy and his father are sad and grieving at the loss of his mother. Tina and Tommy form a strong relationship, opening each other's eyes to the world and taking each other a step closer to fulfilling their dreams.

ALL THOSE WHO...: THINKING ABOUT CHARACTERS' LIVES

Invite students to play the game All Those Who... In this game, students sit in a circle and the teacher asks them if any of the following statements are true for them. If a statement is true for a student, that student stands and changes chairs anyone else who is standing.

I would spread the cloths under your feet
But I, being poor, have only my dreams;
I have spread my dreams beneath your feet;
Tread softly because you tread on my dreams.....

—William Butler Yeats from "He Wishes for Cloths of Heaven"

- All those who have relatives who live outside this country.
- All those who have visited relatives in their country.
- All those who have lived in cities other than where they live now.
- All those who have ever lived outside of this country.
- All those who know someone who has a disability.
- All those who have helped someone achieve a goal/dream.

Invite the students to choose one of the facts that pertained to them and share the story of this fact with a partner.

MEETING THE CHARACTERS/MEETING THE TEXT

Distribute short scenes with the same characters that reveal different information about the play and the characters (see page 163 for examples from *Rice Boy*). Using different scenes will encourage the students to watch and listen to the scenes to learn more about their characters.

Excerpts from *Rice Boy* by Sunil Kuruvilla

#1

TOMMY: Who are you?

TINA: Your cousin. You don't know that?

TOMMY: Your name?

TINA: I'm getting married.

TOMMY: How old are you?

TINA: How old are you?

TOMMY: Twelve

TINA: Ha! I'm seventeen. Eighteen almost.

TOMMY: Your legs are weird.

TINA: They don't work.

TOMMY: I can see everything from up here.

TINA: What do you see?

TOMMY: A fish seller is riding his bicycle. Some men are pushing a taxi. A boy is running beside a tire, slapping it with a stick.

TINA: What does the river look like?

TOMMY: I don't know. Water.

TINA: No, look.

TOMMY: It's dirty

TINA: Keep talking.

#2

TOMMY: I've never climbed a tree before. They aren't this big in Canada.

TINA: Are people swimming?

TOMMY: Some.

TINA: How many?

TOMMY: Four. Four men.

TINA: How far is it from here?

TOMMY: I'm tired.

TINA: No, describe. Keep going. What do the houses look like? Are they different from this one? You can be my eyes. How wide is the road? What do the buses look like? And the trucks? They paint big names on the front, don't they? I've heard them drive by all my life.

TOMMY: You've never seen a truck!

TINA: I've never left this house.

#3

TOMMY: I don't remember the last trip.

TINA: Your mother died. You don't remember that.

TOMMY: I was too little.

TINA: Stupid Boy.

TOMMY: I can see the whole world. What can you see?

TINA: Stop talking.

TOMMY: I see the sari store, the water fountain, the post office.

TINA: Stop it.

TOMMY: I see chickens running through the church. I see the powder factory and butcher shop. I see your mother talking to some man. Can you see the powder factory? Smart Girl, what can you see?

It is best to distribute scenes equally so that the same number of students work on the same scenes; e.g. in a class of 24, each of three scenes will be explored by eight students (four pairs).

Students can read the scenes out loud in the following ways:

1. *Independently:* Students read the scene silently. Students walk through the room and read the scene (both parts) aloud, beginning anywhere but the first line to avoid reading in unison. Students move through the room to find a partner with the same scene, and partners begin working together.
2. *In pairs:* Working in pairs of A and B, A partners read the lines of one character, and B partners read the other character. On a signal from the teacher, they switch roles, but continue reading from where they left off. Continue as the students read through the scene several times.
3. *Practicing different roles:* Students read the scene in a variety of ways—walking together through the room; sitting back-to-back; walking away from each other and then walking toward each other; playing tag as they read; making eye contact; avoiding eye contact—and always changing roles. Students then decide which part they will play through rehearsal and performance.

The students are provided with an opportunity to discuss the following with those who have worked on the same scenes:

- What do we know for sure?
- What do we think we know?
- What do we want to know?

ENTERING THE THEATRE WORLD: REHEARSING THE SCRIPT

Students create a working set, using the furniture in the room, and go through the scene in the set several times.

Each group finds a partner group with a different excerpt and shares their scenes. They discuss the new information gathered from watching the scenes.

Students return to their home groups and share the new information. They record the information on graphic organizer: *What we know for sure/What we think we know/What we want to know.* The groups observe one or two other scenes so they bring different information to the discussion.

Ask the students to take this new information to their scenes and revise, making changes to staging, set, character. Students continue to rehearse.

You can choose strategies from the Strategy Scheme on page 157 to encourage students to continue to revisit the scene with new perspectives and objectives.

A CHARACTER'S DAY: IMPROVISATION

Students are divided into two groups according to the characters they play, and are asked to think about the character's day, hour by hour. Working with scenes from *Rice Boy:* the character of Tommy can consider Tommy's life in Canada so that Tina might come to know more about life in Canada; students playing Tina can consider what she might do all day, given that she does not leave the house.

Invite students in one role (Tina) to mime a day in the character's life, as the students in the role of the other character (Tommy) observe. As you call out the hours, the students mime the activities of the character from 8 am through until midnight. At the end, the students in role of the observer discuss what they have learned about the other character from observing her day; e.g., *What have you learned about Tina? Have your feelings towards her changed through observing her day? How will this affect your portrayal of Tommy in the scene?* The observers then create their day in mime, hour by hour, and the students in role of the other character comment on what they learned about the character.

BUILDING A COMPOSITE CHARACTER

Students playing the same roles work in small groups and discuss the character. Ask the students to begin the discussion by sharing their favorite lines in the scene—the line they like saying and that they feel represents the essence of the character. Students justify their choices.

Invite the students to combine their ideas and thoughts to create a sculpture of the character that represents the inside and outside feelings. Students then add their selected lines, deciding on an order and presentation of the words.

Students share their character collages. They can share all of one character first and then the other, or they can move from character to character.

Reflection

Ask students how this activity deepens their understanding of the characters.
• What do you think the character is thinking and feeling on the inside?
• How do these characters feel about each other?
• What can they do to help each other?

SCENE STUDY

Students return to their partners to revise and edit their scenes based on the learning from the group explorations. They can add props, costume pieces. While they are rehearsing, on a signal from the teacher, students freeze in the moment and consider, as the character, any of the following prompts:

• I really want…
• I want her/him to understand…
• I feel...
• I dream...

These prompts could lead to monologues or writing in role.

The teacher calls upon individual students to complete the prompt aloud.

PRESENTATION/PERFORMANCE

Students are organized into groups of six, so all three scenes are included in each group. Together the group considers how they will negotiate to present the scenes by considering the following:

• Voice
• Entrances and exits of characters
• Transitions
• Gesture and movement
• Creation of single set
• Use of furniture and props
• Opening and closing images
• Lighting
• Use of levels
• Blocking (arrangement of people)

- Music
- Position of audience

Each group has an opportunity to stage and present their scenes.

There are many ways to present scenes in class. For classes that struggle with memorizing lines, students can present a snippet or the essence of each scene in a tableau. Scenes can be performed chronologically; scenes can be broken up; lines and moments can be repeated. It is important that students consider transitions to make moving from scene to scene seamless. Students can present their scenes in chronological order or negotiate another order that would work to convey meaning.

Reflection

- How did rehearsing and presenting the scenes help you understand these characters?
- In what way are the stagings similar or different?
- What advice might you give to the group to improve their presentation?
- What did you enjoy about another group's presentation that you would consider incorporating into your own work?
- What did you most enjoy about the process of interpreting, rehearsing, and presenting scenes?

CULMINATING ACTIVITY: DREAMS

Students work in groups to create a dream that each character (or both) might have. This dream will depict an optimistic view of their future. Dreams can presented using tableaux, movement, slow motion, soundscape, song, etc. Students can complete sentence stems (see page 156) in the role of a character to prepare them for the dream activity. Dreams can be incorporated into a presentation of the three scenes—before, between, or after the presentation of the scenes.

I need him so badly. I don't want him to go away! Sometimes, just sometimes I dream about him. I dream…

—Michel Tremblay from *Les Belles Soeurs*

Assessment: Rubric for Scene Study

Criteria	Emerging	Limited	Considerable	Consistently
Performance demonstrates understanding and analysis of character (authentic, detailed, engaging)				
Role is sustained throughout the performance; concentration is evident				
Voice is audible, expressive of character				
Lines are memorized, integrated in the role				
Technology (lighting, music) used to reveal character, tension, situation				
Set and props, costume transitions reveal understanding of character and context (situation)				

Pembroke Publishers ©2010 *Drama Schemes, Themes & Dreams* by Larry Swartz and Debbie Nyman ISBN 978-1-55138-253-1

Self Assessment: Interpretation and Communication

Name: _____ Date: _____

A. Check the box that shows how you feel about the following statements:

	Agree	Neither Agree nor Disagree	Disagree
1. I enjoy interpreting scripts.	☐	☐	☐
2. I enjoyed working with different partners/small groups to explore scripts.	☐	☐	☐
3. I investigated a variety of possibilities for using voice, gesture, and movement to read scripts out loud	☐	☐	☐
4. I often contributed ideas in interpreting scripts, directing scenes, and presenting scripts.	☐	☐	☐
5. I followed directions and accepted advice from others.	☐	☐	☐
6. I understand the significance of revising/rehearsing.	☐	☐	☐
7. I worked effectively in role to interpret scripts.	☐	☐	☐
8. I was engaged with/committed to interpretation activities.	☐	☐	☐

B. Answer the following questions:

1. Which interpretation activity appealed to you most? Why?

2. Which do you prefer: watching others role-play a character or taking part in a role-play? Why?

3. What did you learn about yourself by interpreting scripts?

4. What did you learn about working with scripts in this unit?

5. What aspect(s) of your interpretation work would you like to improve?

Pembroke Publishers ©2010 *Drama Schemes, Themes & Dreams* by Larry Swartz and Debbie Nyman ISBN 978-1-55138-253-1

Recommended Resources

Professional Resources

Ames, R. S. (2005) *A High School Theatre Teacher's Survival Guide*. New York, NY: Routledge.

Baldwin, P. (2009) *School Improvement Through Drama*. London, UK: Network Continuum. London, UK: David Fulton Publishers.

Battye, S. (ed.) (2010) *Drama Cuts*. Sydney, AU: Phoenix Education.

—(2007) *With Drama in Mind*. London, UK: Network Continuum.

Booth, D. (2005) *Story Drama: Reading, writing and role-playing across the curriculum*. Markham, ON: Pembroke Publishers.

Booth, D., & B Barton (2000) *Story Works*. Markham, ON: Pembroke Publishers.

Booth, D., & M. Hachiya (2004) *The Arts Go To School*. Markham, ON: Pembroke Publishers.

Booth, D., & C. Lundy (1985) *Improvisation*. Toronto, ON: Nelson Publishers.

———— (1983) *Interpretation*. Toronto, ON: Nelson Publishers.

Bowell, P., & B. Heap (2001) *Planning Process Drama*.

Carroll, J., M. Anderson & D. Cameron (2006) *Real Players? Drama, technology and education*. Trent, UK: Trentham Books.

Clark, J., W. Dobson, T. Goode & J. Neelands (1997) *Lessons for the Living: Drama and the integrated curriculum*. Newmarket, ON: Mayfair Cornerstone Limited.

Dodson, R., (ed.) (2009) *Arts at the Heart: A practical guide to dance and drama in the elementary schools*. Stratford, ON: Drama Focus Arts Consulting Group.

Eriksson, S. A. (2009) *Distancing at Close Range: Investigating the significance of distancing in drama education. Bergen, Norway*: Contact stig.erikssson@hib.no s-erikss@online.no

Fels, L. G. Belliveau (2008) *Exploring Curriculum: Performative Inquiry, Role Drama, and learning*. Vancouver, BC: Pacific Educational Press.

Gallagher, K. (2007) *The Theatre of Urban: Youth and schooling in dangerous times*. Toronto, ON: University of Toronto Press.

—(2000) *Drama Education in the Lives of Girls: Imagining Possibilities*. Toronto, ON: University of Toronto Press.

—& D. Booth. (eds.) (2003) *How Theatre Educates: Convergences and counterpoints*. Toronto, ON: University of Toronto Press.

Ginnis, P. & S. (2006). *Covering the Curriculum With Stories*. Carmatheren, Wales: Crown House Press.

Glossop, J. (2007) *Directing: The art and craft*. Self-published.

Hulson, M. (2006) *Schemes for Classroom Drama*. Trent, UK: Trentham Books.

Johnson, L., & C O'Neill (1984) *Dorothy Heathcote: Collected writings on education and drama*. London, UK: Hutchinson.

Lundy, K. G. (2008) *Teaching Fairly in an Unfair World*. Markham, ON: Pembroke Publishers.

—(2007) *Leap Into Literacy*. Markham, ON: Pembroke Publishers.

—(2004) *What Do I Do About the Kid Who…?* Markham, ON: Pembroke Publishers.

Morgan, N. & J. Saxton. (2006) *Asking Better Questions*. Markham, ON: Pembroke Publishers.

Neelands, J. (1998) *Beginning Drama 11-14*. London, UK: David Fulton Publishers.

Neelands, J & T. Goode (2000) *Structuring Drama Work: A handbook of available forms in theatre and drama*. Cambridge, UK: Cambridge University Press.

O'Connor, P. (ed.) (2010) *Creating Democratic Citizenship Through Drama Education: The writings of Jonothan Neelands*. Trent, UK: Trentham Books

O'Neill, C. (1995) *Drama Worlds: A framework for Process Drama*. Portsmouth, NH: Heinemann.

Prendergast, M. & J. Saxton (2010) *Applied Theatre: International case studies and challenges for practice*. Bristol, UK: Intellect Ltd.

Pura, T. (2002) *Stages: Creative Ideas for Teaching Drama*. Winnepeg, MA: J. Gordon Shillingford Publications.

Swados, E. (2006) *At Play: Teaching teenagers theatre*. New York, NY: Faber and Faber.

Swartz, L (2002) *The New Dramathemes*. Markham, ON: Pembroke Publishers.

Taylor, P. & C.D. Warner (2006) *Structure and Spontaneity: The process drama of Cecily O'Neill*. Trent, UK: Trentham Books.

Tough, Paul (2009) "The Make-Believe Solution" in *The New York Times Magazine*, September.

Wooland, Brian (2008) *Pupils as Playwrights: Drama, Literacy and playwriting*. Trent, UK: Trentham Books.

Chapter 1

FOLKTALES

Barton, Bob; Illus. Jirina Martin (2003) *The Bear Says North: Tales from Northern Lands*.

Coates, Lucy (2002) *The Boy Who Fell From the Sky*.

Helmer, Marilyn (2001) *Three Tales of Enchantment*.

James, Elizabeth; Illus. Atanas (2008) *The Woman Who Married A Bear*.

Martin, Rafe; Illus. David Shannon (1992) *The Rough-Face Girl*.

— (1996) *The Boy Who Lived with Seals*.

Nauwald, Nana (2004) *Flying with Shamans*.

San Souci, Robert D. (1994) *Sootface: An Ojibway Cinderella Story*.

Taylor, C. J. (2009) *Spirits, Fairies and Merpeople*

NOVELS

Clemens, Andrew (2002) *Things Not Seen* (sequel: *Things Hoped For*).

Cody, Matthew (2009) *Powerless*.

Davis, Terry (retold) ; Illus. Dennis Calero (2008) *The Invisible Man*.

Fisher, Catherine (2010) *Incarceron*.

Kuhlman, Evan; Illus. J.P. Coovert (2008) *The Last Invisible Boy*.

Rivers, Karen (2008) *What Z Sees (The XYZ Trilogy)*.

Rowling, J.K. (1997) Harry Potter series.

Matas, Carol (1997) The Freak series.

Meyers, Stephanie (2005) The Twilight Saga.

Wyndham, John (1955) *The Chrysalids*.

Chapter 2

NOVELS FEATURING ADOLESCENT OUTCASTS

Anderson, Laurie Halse (1999) *Speak*.

Cameron, Peter (2007) *Someday this Pain Will Be Useful to You*.

Chbosky, Stephen (1999) *The Perks of Being a Wallflower*.

Cormier, Robert (1974) *The Chocolate War*.

Draper, Sharon M. (2010) *Out of My Mind*.

Flake, Sharon G. (1998) *The Skin I'm In*.

Giles, Gail (2002) *Shattering Glass*.

Hopkins, Ellen (2007) *Burned* (also: *Crank*).

Howe, James (2001) *The Misfits*.

McCormick, Patricia (2002) *Cut*.

Myers, Walter Dean (1999) *Monster*.

Myracle, Lauren (2008) Internet Girls series: *l8r, g8r, ttfn, ttyl*.

Schmidt. Gary D (2008) *Trouble* (also: *The Wednesday Wars*).

Spinelli, Jerry (2000) *Stargirl* (sequel: *Love, Stargirl*).

van de Ruit, John (2005) *Spud*.

SCRIPTS

Ardal, Maja (2006) *You Fancy Yourself*.

Foon, Dennis (1989/2003) *Mirror Game*.

Foon, Dennis (1988) *Skin and Liars*.

Thomson, Kristen (2001) *I, Claudia* (also on DVD).

Judith Thompson (2010) *Such Creatures*.

Wade, Bryan (2006) *Brave New Playwrights: Highlights of UBC's creative writing department*

Chapter 3

NOVELS

Almond, David; Illus. Dave McKean (2008) *The Savage*.

Bloor, Edward (1997) *Tangerine*.

Chambers, Aidan (1983) *The Present Takers*.

Gardner, Graham (2003) *Inventing Elliot*.

Herrick, Steven (2007) *The Wolf*.

Howe, James (2001) *The Misfits*.

Koss, Amy Goldman (2006) *Poison Ivy*.

Masters, Anthony (1995) *Bullies Don't Hurt*.

Pignat, Caroline (2008) *Egghead*.

Prose, Francine (2007) *Bullyville*.

Singer, Nicky (2001) *Feather Boy*.

Spinelli, Jerry (2002) *Loser*.

— (1997) *Wringer*.

Strasser, Todd (1999) *Give a Boy a Gun*.

SCRIPTS

Brooks, Martha and Maureen Hunter (1995) *I Met a Bully on the Hill*.

Foon, Dennis (1993) *Seesaw* (Also: *War*).

Kaufman, Moises (2001) *The Laramie Project*.

MacLeod, Joan (2002) *The Shape of A Girl*.

REFERENCE MATERIALS

Artz, Sibylle (1998) *Sex, Power and the Violent School Girl*. Toronto, ON: Trifolium Books.

Coloroso, Barbara (2002) *The Bully, The Bullied and the Bystander*. New York, NY: HarperCollins.

— (2005) *Just Because It's Not Wrong Doesn't Make it Right: From toddlers to teens, teaching kids to think and act ethically*. New York, NY: HarperCollins.

Ellis, Deborah (2010) *We Want You to Know: Kids talk about Bullying*. Regina, SK: Coteau Books.

Gardner, Olivia (2008) *Letters to a Bullied Girl: Messages of healing and hope.* New York, NY: HarperCollins.

Garbarino, James and Ellen deLara (2002) *And Words Can Hurt Forever: How to protect adolescents from bullying, harassment and emotional violence.* New York, NY: Simon & Schuster.

Lundy, Kathleen Gould (2008) *Teaching Fairly in an Unfair World.* Markham, ON: Pembroke Publishers.

National Film Board (2004) *It's a Girl's World.* Toronto, ON: NFB (DVD)

Perlman, Janet (2000) *Bully Dance.* Toronto, ON: NFB (DVD)

Simmons, Rachel (2002) *Odd Girl Out: The hidden culture of aggression in girls:* New York, NY: Harcourt Inc.

Swartz, Larry and Kathy Broad (2004).*Sticks and Stones.* Toronto, ON: Rubicon Publishers/Nelson Publishers

Chapter 4

GRAPHIC NOVELS

Avi (1993) *City of Light, City of Dark.*

Crocci, Pascal (2003) *Auschwitz.*

Cutting, Robert; Illus. Jeremy Bennison (2009) *Shadow World.*

Hotta, Yumi (2004) Hikuru No Go series.

Green, Joan and Kathleen Gould Lundy (various dates) Bold-print Graphic Novels series.

Myers, Christopher and Christopher Myers (2005) *Autobiography of My Dead Brother.*

Phelan, Matt (2009) *The Storm in the Barn.*

Satrapi, Marjane (2003) *Persepolis: The story of a childhood.*

Selznick, Brian (2007) *The Invention of Hugo Cabret.*

Small, David (2009) *Stitches.*

Smith, Jeff (2006) Bone series.

Spiegelman, Art (1973) *Maus* (sequel: *Maus II*).

Tamaki, Mariko; Illus. Jillian Tamaki (2008) *Skim.*

Tan, Shaun (2007) *The Arrival.*

Townsend, Michael (2010) *Amazing Greek Myths of Wonders and Blunders.*

Vieceli, Emma (Illus) (2007) *Hamlet* (Manga Shakespeare series).

Watts, Irene N.; Illus. Kathryn E. Shoemaker (2009) *Good-Bye Marianne.*

Yang, Gene Luen (2006) *American Born Chinese.*

REFERENCES

Booth, David and Kathleen Gould Lundy (2007) *In Graphic Detail.* Markham, ON: Scholastic. (also: *Boosting Literacy with Graphic Novels.* Austin, TX: Steck Vaughn.)

Cary, Stephen (2004) *Going Graphic.* Portsmouth, NH: Heineman.

Thompson, Terry (2008) *Adventures in Graphica: Using comics and graphic novels to teach comprehension,* 2-6. Portland, ME: Stenhouse.

Chapter 5

NOVELS

Curtis, Paul Christopher (2007) *Elijah of Buxton.*

Lester, Julius (2005) *Days of Tears.*

Paterson, Katherine (1997/2005) *Jip: His Story.*

Paulsen, Gary (1993) *Night John* (sequel: *Sarny*).

Schwartz, Virginia Frances (2002) *If I Just Had Two Wings.*

Smucker, Barbara (1977/2009) *Underground to Canada.*

POETRY ANTHOLOGIES

Rappaport, Doreen; Illus. Shane W. Evans (2004) *Free at Last! Stories and Songs of Emancipation.*

Rochelle, Belinda (ed.) (2001) *Words with Wings: An anthology of African-American Poetry and Art.*

Weatherford, Carole Boston (2002) *Remember the Bridge: Poems of a people.*

PICTURE BOOKS

Edwards, Pamela Duncan (1998) *Barefoot.*

Hamilton, Virginia; Illus. Leo and Diane Dillon (1985/2004) *The People Could Fly.*

Levine, Ellen; Illus. Kadir Nelson (2002) *Henry's Freedom Box: A true story from the Underground Railroad.*

Morrison, Tony (2004) *Remember: The journey to school integration.*

Raven, Margot Theis; Illus. E.B. Lewis (2008) *Night Boat to Freedom.*

Weatherford, Carole Boston; Illus. Kadir Nelson (2006) *Moses: When Harriet Tubman Led Her People to Freedom.*

Woodson, Jacqueline; Illus Hudson Talbott (2005) *Show Way.*

Chapter 6

Johnstone, Keith (1992) *Impro: Improvisation and theatre.*

PICTURE BOOKS

Hoffman, Mary; Illus. Karen Littlewood (2002) *The Color of Home.*

Machizuki, Ken; Illus. Dom Lee (2003) *Passage to Freedom: The Sugihira Story.*

Robinson, Anthony, Annemarie Young and June Allan (2010) *Mohammad's Journey: A refugee's diary* (Also: *Hamzat's Journey, Gervelie's Journey*).

Williams, Karen Lynn and Khadra Mohammad; Illus. Catherine Stock (2004) *My Name is Sangoel.*

—: Illus. Doug Chayka (2007) *Four Feet, Two Sandals.*

NOVELS

Applegate, Katherine (2007) *Home of the Brave*.
Burg. Ann E. (2009) *All the Broken Pieces*.
Holm, Ann (1963/2003) *I am David*
Paterson, Katherine (2009) *The Day of the Pelican*.
Stine, Catherine (2006) *Refugees*.

NONFICTION

Bixler, Mark (2005) *Lost Boys of Sudan: An American Story of the Refugee Experience*.
Bradman, Tony (ed.) (2007) *Give Me Shelter: Stories about children who seek asylum*.
Clacherty, Glynis (2008) *The Suitcase Stories: Refugee Children Reclaim Their Identities*
Dalton, Dave (2006) *Refugee & Asylum Seekers*.
Ellis, Deborah (2009) *Children of War: Voices of Iraqi refugees*.
Goode, Katherine (2004) *Jumping to Heaven: Stories about Refugee Children*.
Naidoo, Beverley (ed.) (2004) *Making it Home: Real-life stories from children forced to flee*.
St. John, Warren (2009) *Outcasts United: A refugee team, an American Town*.

WEBSITES

www.unrefugees.org
www.refugeeresearch.net

Chapter 7

PICTURE BOOKS

Bunting, Eve; Illus. Peter Sylvada (2001) *Gleam and Glow*.
_____ : Illus. Ronald Himler (1992) *The Wall*.
Cali, Davide: Illus. Serge Bloch (2009) *The Enemy*.
Crew, Gary: Illus. Shaun Tan (2004) *Memorial*.
Croci, Pascal (2002) *Auschwitz*.
Foreman, Michael (2009) *A Child's Garden*.
Hesse, Karen; Illus. Wendy Watson (2004) *The Cats in Krasinski Square*.
Huggins-Cooper, Lynn; Illus. Ian Benfold Haywood (2008) *One Boy's War*.
Innocenti, Robert (1985) *Rose Blanche*.
Lobel, Anita (1967/2004) *Potatoes Potatoes*.
McKee, David (2004) *The Conquerers*.
McPhail, David (2009) *No!*
Morpurgo, Michael; Illus. Laura Carlin (2009) *The Kites Are Flying!*
Radunsky, V. (2004) *What Does Peace Look Like?*
Skarmeta, Antonio; Illus. Alfonso Ruano (1998) *The Composition*.

Stamaty, Mark Alan (2004) *Alia's Mission: Saving the books of Iraq*
Tsuchiya, Yukio (1951/1988) *Faithful Elephants*.
Vaugelade, Anais (2001) *The War*.
Winter, Jeanette (2003) *The Librarian of Basra*.
Zee, Ruth Vander; Illus. Roberto Innocenti (2003) *Erika's Story*.

POETRY

Bennett, Jill (ed.) (2001) *Peace Begins With Me*.
Greenfield, Eloise; Illus. Jan Spivey Gilchrist (2006) *When the Horses Ride By: Children in times of war*.
Marsden, John (1997/2005) *Prayer for the twenty-first century*.
Robb, Laura (ed.); Illus. Debra Lill (1997) *Music and Drum*.

NOVELS

Avi (1984) *The Fighting Ground*.
Keller, Julia (2009) *Back Home*.
McCormick, Patricia (2009) *Purple Heart*.
Gleitzman, Morris (2005) *Once* (sequel *Then*).
Myers, Walter Dean (2008) *Sunrise Over Fallujah* (Also: *Fallen Angels*).
Morpurgo, Michael (2003) *Private Peaceful*.
_____ (1982/ 2004) *War Horse*.
Paterson, Katherine (1989) *Park's Quest*.
Paulsen, Gary (2010) *Woods Runner*.
_____ (1998) *Soldier's Heart*.
Walters, Eric (2009) *Wounded*.
Zenatti, Valérie (2005/2008) *A Bottle in the Gaza Sea*.

SCRIPTS

Gray, John and Eric Peterson (1976/2009) *Billy Bishop Goes to War*.
Levine, Karen; Sher Emil (2002/2006) *Hana's Suitcase on Stage*.
Littlewood, Joan (1963/1996) *Oh! What a Lovely War*.
Mouawad, Wajdi (2005) *Scorched*.
Reade, Simon (2006) *Private Peaceful: Based on the novel by Michael Morpurgo*.
Murrell, John (1977) *Waiting for the Parade*.
Rogers, J.T. (2007) *The Overwhelming*.
Stafford, Nick (2007) *War Horse: Based on the novel by Michael Morpurgo*.
Thomson, Judith (2008) *Palace of the End*.
Viner, Katherine and Alan Rickman (eds.) (2005) *My Name is Rachel Corrie*.
Slobodzianek, Tadeusz (2004/ 2009) *Our Class*.

NONFICTION

Armstrong, Jennifer (2002) *Shattered: Stories of children and war*.

Aronson, Marc and Patty Campbell (eds.) (2008) *War Is... Soldiers, survivors and storytellers talk about war.*

Granfield, Linda; Illus Janet Stevens (2000) *In Flanders Fields: The story of the poem by John McCrea* (Also: *Where Poppies Grow; A World War I Companion; High Flight: A story of World War II; I Remember Korea: Veterans tell their stories of the Korean War*).

Ellis, Deborah (2008) *Off to War: Voices of Soldiers' Children.*

Halilbegovich, Nadja (2006) *My Childhood Under Fire: A Sarajevo Diary.*

Kacer, Kathy and Sharon E. McKay (2010) *Whispers in Hiding.*

Morpurgo, Michael (ed.) (2006) *War: Stories of conflict.*

Palmer, Laura (1988) *Shrapnel of the Heart: Letters and remembrances from the Vietnam Veterans Memorial.*

SONGS

"Blowin' in the Wind" (Bob Dylan)
"Bring Him Home" (from *Les Miserables*)
"Bring Them Home" (Bruce Springstein)
"Earth Song" (Michael Jackson)
"From a Distance" (Bette Midler)
"Give Peace a Chance" (John Lennon)
"Hallelujah" (Leonard Cohen)
"I Ain't a-Marchin' Anymore" (Phil Ochs)
"Imagine" (John Lennon)
"One Tin Soldier" (Original Cast)
"Sons" (Jacques Brel)
"Sunday Bloody Sunday" (U2)
"Universal Soldier" (Buffy St. Marie)
"Where Have All the Flowers Gone?" (Pete Seeger)

Chapter 8

TOP TEN SCRIPTS FOR YOUNG ADOLESCENTS RECOMMENDED BY THEATREBOOKS (With thanks to John Harvey and Leonard McHardy)

Fleischman, Paul (2005) *Zap.*

Foon Dennis (1989) *New Canadian Kid / Invisible Kids* (Also: *Skin/ Liars*).

Gaudreault, Jean-Rock (translated by Linda Gaboriau) (2005) *Mathew and Stephen.*

Johnson, Marcia (2010) *Binti's Journey* (based on the novel *The Heaven Shop* by Deborah Ellis).

Kaufman, Moises (2001) *The Laramie Project.*

Kuruvilla, Sunil (2009) *Rice Boy.*

Lazarus, John and Judith Marcuse (2000) *ICE: Beyond Cool.*

Martini, Clem (2006) *Illegal Entry.*

Sher, Emil (2002/2006) *Hana's Suitcase on Stage* (original story by Karen Levine)

Walker, George F. (1993/ 2007) *Tough.*

SCENES AND MONOLOGUES

Ferry, David (2007) *He Speaks: Monologues for Men.*

Lane, Eric and Nina Shengold (eds.) (1997) *Take Ten: New 10-Minute plays.*

Slaight, Craig and Jack Sharrar (eds.) (1995) *Multicultural Scenes for Young Actors.*

Thompson, Judith (2004) *She Speaks: Monologues for Women.*

Iris Turkott and Keith Turnbull (2006) *Canada on Stage: Scenes and monologues.*

Blizzard Publishing (2004) *Instant Applause: Twenty-nine very short complete plays.*

Surface Mary Hall (2000) *Short Scenes and Monologues for Middle School Actors* (Also: *More Short Scenes and Monologues for Middle School Actors*)

These credits/permissions constitute an extension of the copyright page.

Page 34: from *Skin* by Dennis Foon, copyright © by Dennis Foon; page 159: from *Alphonse* by Wajdi Mouawad, translated by Shelley Tepperman, copyright © 2002 by Shelley Tepperman; page 163: from *Rice Boy* by Sunil Kuruvilla, copyright © 2009 by Sunil Kuruvilla; all reprinted by permission of Playwrights Canada Press. Page 61: "Mosquito" by Larry Swartz from *Sticks and Stones*, Boldprint, reprinted by permission Rubicon Publishers. Page 62: "Under Attack" by Peter Jalaill from *This Healing Place and Other Poems*, reprinted by permission of the author. Page 65: Tracey Blance: "Shame", *Orbit* Magazine, Vol. 34, Number 2, 2004. Page 83: from *Persepolis: The Story of a Childhood* by Marjane Satrapi, © 2003, reprinted by permission Random House, Inc. Page 126: "Operation Stork Winds Down" by Jane Taber, *The Globe and Mail*, January 29, 2010; page 139: "Dear Sweetheart" *The Globe and Mail*; both © CTVglobemedia Publishing, Inc. All rights reserved. Page 130: from *Leaving Home* in The Mercer Trilogy, copyright © 2009 David French, reprinted by permission of Anansi Press. Page 135: City of Vancouver Archives, LP 109, photographer Claude Dettloff. Page 138: *The Enemy* book jacket illustration © 2009 by Serge Bloch, reprinted by permission of Schwartz & Wade Books.

Index